# Holy Disunity

# Holy Disunity

## How What Separates Us Can Save Us

Layton E. Williams

WESTMINSTER
JOHN KNOX PRESS
LOUISVILLE · KENTUCKY

*First edition*
Published by Westminster John Knox Press
Louisville, Kentucky

19 20 21 22 23 24 25 26 27 28—10 9 8 7 6 5 4 3 2 1

Scripture quotations are from the New Revised Standard Version of the Bible, copyright © 1989 by the Division of Christian Education of the National Council of the Churches of Christ in the U.S.A., and are used by permission.

*Book design by Sharon Adams*
*Cover design by Stephen Brayda*

**Library of Congress Cataloging-in-Publication Data**
Names: Williams, Layton E., author.
Title: Holy disunity : how what separates us can save us / Layton E. Williams.
Description: First edition. | Louisville, Kentucky : Westminster John Knox Press, 2019. | Includes bibliographical references.
Identifiers: LCCN 2019005262 (print) | ISBN 9780664265663 (pbk. : alk. paper)
Subjects: LCSH: Church controversies. | Conflict management—Religious aspects—Christianity. | Interpersonal relations—Religious aspects—Christianity.
Classification: LCC BV652.9 .W53 2019 (print) | LCC BV652.9 (ebook) | DDC 262/.8—dc23
LC record available at https://lccn.loc.gov/2019005262
LC ebook record available at https://lccn.loc.gov/2019981087

Most Westminster John Knox Press books are available at special quantity discounts when purchased in bulk by corporations, organizations, and special-interest groups. For more information, please email SpecialSales@wjkbooks.com.

*Dedicated to my family.*

*My family of origin: by birth, by law, and by love.*

*And my family of choice: by circumstance,
by divine care, and by sheer luck.*

*You have all loved me into who I am. And you all remind
me daily that the messy, hard, complicated, beautiful,
tension-filled, imperfect, dusty road is always worth
taking, and it's always the one that leads home.*

# Contents

# Foreword

Too often, people of faith deride theology as "ivory-tower," meaning that it is irrelevant and disconnected from real life. Indeed, too much theology is an academic production, meant more for specialized journals and tenure committees than for people struggling to live God's hopes and dreams in the world.

That, of course, is a bit of cultural stereotype. Through the centuries, the most compelling Christian theology has been written by women and men on the front lines of doubt, protest, and persecution. We often forget that Luther wrote much of his work while hiding from authorities, that Calvin penned the *Institutes* on horseback trying to escape capture by his opponents. Most great women theologians of the Middle Ages, like Hildegard of Bingen, Teresa of Avila, and Sor Juana de la Cruz, were suspected of heresy—an accusation that continues to be hurled at contemporary female theologians—and were brought up on charges, silenced, or threatened with prison. Theologians we now find inspiring examples—like Oscar Romero or Martin Luther King or Dorothy Day or Simone Weil—were nothing less than troublemakers when they were alive. We think of all these writers as "famous" now: distant, learned, and saintly.

But the truth of the matter is that they were just people, women and men with hopes and passions, who took to the streets with those dreams and wrote well about God and the sacred call of mercy, love, and justice. As far as I know, not one lived in an ivory tower. Instead, most lived on the edge of communities, often kicked to the curb by their own people, and used their voices to cry out against the evils of their own days.

No doubt Layton Williams will be embarrassed by a recitation of this litany of saints at the beginning of her book. But I bring them up to remind readers of a very important thing: Theology is the job of God's people—all the unexpected, not famous people who are living their faith in difficult days and who take the risk to reflect on Jesus and grace and goodness and dare to put their words in the world to inspire or critique or what have you. Being a theologian is a by-product of life. And the most memorable, world-transforming theologies are written by those who live on edges, who find themselves at the borders of communities, who get kicked out or thrown out of families or churches, and who are always making trouble by turning over conventions and questioning the normal ways of doing things. People who don't really fit. They are Christianity's most needed theologians.

That is what I found in these pages. A young, fresh, unexpected theological voice—a woman who (admittedly) doesn't fit anywhere—taking on one of modern Christianity's most cherished ideals: unity. Reverend Williams dusts off the tropes of ecumenism with wit and intelligence, arguing that real unity isn't something we can do because unity is ultimately something God does for us. Even worse than thinking we can create unity, our pretensions to and plans for unity are actually dividing us ever more deeply. We've turned God's gift into an idol. Sound familiar? It should. That is one of the central stories in the biblical narrative.

Williams asks us to let go of the idol of unity, and to see what is holy in disunity. She points out how difference, doubt, argument, tension, separation, vulnerability, trouble, protest, hunger, limitations, failure, and uncertainty form a way of realistic spirituality. This doesn't end in some Christian utopia, but does make the world a better, more humane, and more kindly place.

At this historical moment, Christian theology is awash in grand schemes. And that might be the problem with all our churches, both liberal and conservative. It seems that a humble and harder way toward a sustainable communal life here in this world is what we need most. *Holy Disunity* is wisdom without hubris. We need it right now.

Diana Butler Bass
Alexandria, Virginia

# Acknowledgments

In some ways, this book seems to have burst into being with all the speed and ferocity of a summer storm in the South. In other ways, it has been the slow work of a lifetime. I am indebted to so many, both those who've storm-chased with me these last months and those who've walked beside me on the long, winding journey.

I am deeply grateful for the people and communities who have encouraged me in faith. My grandmother, Robbie Lou "Nana" Stanfiel Blough, who set an early example of faith that defines how one lives. The Rev. Shannon Dill, who has gamely wrestled questions of life and faith with me from my youth group days to this very moment. And for St. Luke's Presbyterian Church in Dunwoody, UGA Presbyterian Student Center, Central Presbyterian Church in Austin, Austin Presbyterian Theological Seminary (APTS), Parity's "secret queer church camp," Broad Street Ministry in Philadelphia, Fourth Presbyterian in Chicago, Young Clergy Women International, and Sojourners.

I am also grateful for those who have encouraged me in my writing—most of all for my mother, who passed on her own gift to me and then encouraged me to make it my own. And to my dad and stepdad, siblings, and extended family, and my friends (Robin, Lila, Anna, Meredith, my APTS crew, my Sojo folks, and so many others throughout the years) who have supported my devotion to stories all this time. I am grateful, too, to them all for joining me in this hard, messy work of loving in the midst of disunity.

I want to thank my teachers, who are too many to name and whose support and wisdom have been invaluable in getting me here. In particular: Mrs. Kelley, Ms. Parmalee, Mrs. Gustin, Mrs. McDaniel, Mr. Davis, Mr. Cawthon, Mrs. Britten, and Mrs. Jordan—who all saw potential amid my rule-defying, daydream-distracted chaos. Those professors who kept me writing and dreaming in college. And Todd, who I thought was just teaching me improv, but, it turns out, was teaching me much more. And thank you to the entire faculty and staff of APTS, who gave me three incredible years of challenge, wonder, and learning that changed me forever.

Of course, none of this would be possible without those who helped bring this book into being in very tangible ways. Thank you in particular to Austen Hartke, who connected me to my wonderful editor, and to Emmy Kegler, M Barclay, Jessica Kantrowitz, and David Potter—all of whom read, edited, and offered feedback in the earliest stages of this book. And to Brad Lyons and Lisa Kloskin for asking the questions that kept me writing and moving forward. Above all, thank you to Westminster John Knox Press, for recognizing the need for this book and allowing it to become a reality. And especially to Jessica Miller Kelley, for loving it with me, and helping shape and edit it into the best book it could be.

I'm grateful for everyone who shows up in this book, whether by direct reference or simply unspoken connection. I'm so glad life allowed our paths to cross.

Thank you, Gryffindor, for always being by my side.

And always and forever, I give thanks to God: for writing, for love, for life, for hope, and for the indomitable grace which shines even in the heart of disunity.

# Introduction

I have spent my entire life deeply loving people with whom I will never agree. We disagree on politics, on faith, and on some of our core values. Over the last few years I have watched the divisions in our world and especially our country grow deeper and deeper—or perhaps I've merely watched existing divisions come more and more to light. I have observed the conversations becoming both angrier (which I believe is sometimes good, or at least fair) and more hateful (which I believe is neither productive nor good). I've seen, all around me, people retreating into havens of like-minded community, and I have seen their ability to tolerate others—even to recognize that others are human beings beloved and created in the image of God—wither to nothing. For an empathetic, sensitive, and conflict-averse person, it has been agonizing. Most days it feels like the world is on fire and it won't stop burning till everything and everyone is turned to ash.

To my surprise, I have found that my impulse in response to this inflamed reality is not to run and hide, nor to cocoon myself in noncontroversial spaces, nor even to rely on my privilege to tune it all out. Instead, I have felt an overwhelming and irrepressible urge to run into the fire, to dive headfirst into the growing chasm between us all, and do whatever is within my power to repair the breach. To help people remember that even when we hate, God loves, and so when we hate, we hate what God loves

1

and to some degree we hate God. I suppose that I'm driven into the fray because I've got people I love at stake, whom I'm unwilling to let go of, and convictions I'm not willing to let go of either.

I recently moved back to the South after ten years away, specifically to settle in Charleston, South Carolina, close to my family, and do this hard work of living in the breach. I have long articulated my sense of call as "love God's people, and tell the truth," and that is the work I am trying to do in my life, and it's the work I am trying to do in this book.

I imagine you might think, given the above, that I'd be an advocate for unity at all costs. You might picture me standing in the midst of all the conflict and division, begging people to just come to the table and agree to disagree. It'd be reasonable to assume that I'm one of those people who just wants us all to stay together because "I have friends on both ends of the spectrum," as some people say. But I'm not. Quite the opposite. If you are one of those people, that's okay. Welcome! But I hope that you gathered from the title of this book that you are in for an argument.

I care about unity. I believe deeply that we *are* unified in Christ—that all of humanity and all creation, even, are bound up together in God's love. But I don't think that kind of holy unity is ours to create *or* destroy. And I believe the unity that we attempt to create when we think it is in our power is a broken, hollow, and false unity. It's an earthly unity that often demands a delay or denial of justice. It's unity that sometimes asks people to leave huge parts of themselves at the door in exchange for a tenuous and disingenuous belonging. And frankly, I think this kind of earthly unity often denies the validity of people's convictions or undermines their importance. In short, I believe that when we pursue earthly unity at all costs, it becomes for us an idol—a distraction from the greater unity that comes from God. And in fact, I think this sort of unity—which seems to value collective togetherness over genuine complex relationship—is *unholy* and is driving us further and further apart.

I don't really believe the kind of unity God calls for and promises is possible in the world as it is right now. And more importantly, I think that's *okay*. If we trust in the promise that God has it under control, we can let go a little bit. And if we do—if we stop feeling so threatened by disunity and equating it with violence and destruction—we might very well find that it can even be holy. Many of the things that we fear because we believe that they separate us actually have real gifts to offer. The Bible is full of stories that show this to be true.

I don't believe in either-or options, as a general rule. And I very much don't believe that the only options that exist for us in our modern turbulence are to either force ourselves to stay united no matter what or utterly annihilate one another. I believe there's another way. And my particular experiences as a liberal, bisexual, female pastor in a largely conservative southern family that I deeply love have given me particular insights into why and how this other way might be possible.

This book is an argument for how disunity can be holy, and how we can faithfully coexist without being united, at least in any earthly way. Every chapter is dedicated to a challenge that we fear, how it can divide us, and what gifts we can find in it, as shown through the biblical text, my own life, and other modern examples.

I write largely from my own experience and context as a white mainline Protestant Christian, and I recognize that what is true and applicable to such communities may not entirely resonate with others, whether people of color, people who aren't Christian, or folks who aren't mainline Protestants. Still, whoever you are, I hope that within these pages you find words that deeply resonate and words that challenge you. I hope that you walk away with new ideas about how to live faithfully in our current reality. Above all, I hope this book convinces you of what I so deeply believe to be true: it is not unity but relationship to which we are called in this moment, and, with that in mind, it is possible to hold on to both our convictions and one another.

# Chapter One

# The Gift of Difference

I was a weird kid. I'm not an entirely unweird adult, but I was a really weird kid. Those who knew me then could regale you with stories of my humorously awkward and off-kilter behavior. I was a bleeding-heart, exceptionally sensitive, precocious, and rebellious child born into a conservative, disciplined, traditionally religious southern family in Georgia. I was the youngest, an artist and deep thinker. I talked a lot—mostly to adults, had a penchant for imaginary friends, and cried myself to sleep often over the thought that people somewhere in the world were hurting and I couldn't stop it.

I have often thought that I was born missing some internal mechanism that tells a person what is socially appropriate and what will immediately launch you into the social exosphere. Even my best efforts to be cool, popular, or just plain palatable failed spectacularly. I instinctively spoke whatever crossed my mind and, apparently, what crossed my mind was not common thought. I usually didn't realize I'd said or done something weird until the laughter or awkward silences came. And I never seemed to learn from my mistakes, though I certainly tried.

Sometime in adulthood I discovered the Enneagram—a centuries-old system of personality study that identifies nine primary types based on core values and fears.[1] In the description of Type Four—sometimes called the Individualist and other times the Romantic—I found resonance, validation, and self-acceptance. Type Fours build their identity around the sense of difference they feel between themselves and the rest of the world. They worry they'll never be truly understood. They worry even more that there's nothing unique to understand about them at all. It's common for Enneagram Fours to feel that they are missing some piece of being human that everyone else has. In learning this language to describe my own experience, I learned to value the gifts of being different, and it absolutely changed my world.

But at age ten? Or thirteen? All I could feel was the overwhelming weight of not fitting in, not being whatever it was that I was supposed to be. In this regard, school and birthday parties and hobbies were all a constant source of stress and self-doubt. The only exception, the memory of which I feel not just in my mind but in my whole body, was church. Though I was loved by my family, I always felt clearly different, determined as I was to march to my own drum. In that context, whether it was true or not, I tended to interpret my difference as a shortcoming, something to be overlooked, overcome, or compensated for. At my church, I felt so naturally at home that it never even occurred to me to question whether I belonged.

My mom and stepdad joined Saint Luke's Presbyterian Church in a northern suburb of Atlanta when I was six years old. My mom was in Presbyterian Women, taught adult Sunday school, planned Rally Day skits and the annual Sandwich Project. My stepdad taught elementary Sunday school classes for years. They were both elders. These days, half my pastor friends grew up with pastor parents. But as a kid all I knew was that my parents weren't just Presbyterian. They were *super*-Presbyterians. I spent countless hours roaming the halls of my church, relatively unsupervised while my parents attended this, that, or the other committee meeting. I still contend I know the building better than anyone, right down to secret passageways and hidden rooms.

Thanks to my parents' position in the church community, I felt entirely comfortable and at home with the people too. By age eight, I was writing letters to the pastors offering my advice on children's programming and ideas for church-wide picnics. My parents' friends were like surrogate aunts and uncles, their kids like my cousins, my youth pastor some strange blend of mentor, friend, and second mom. My church community was no doubt imperfect—a lesson I would learn more than once in later years—but the message it unquestionably sent to me during the delicate years of my childhood was, "You are loved, exactly as you are."

When I was twelve, the father of my best friend from church died by suicide. He was close friends with my parents too, and I'd spent enough time around him that he felt almost like family, as so many of my parents' church friends did. I had run up to him with my friend at church a week or two before, babbling about one thing or another. My mom and stepdad tried to keep quiet about the news for fear of upsetting me, but when I asked them where they were headed in church clothes on a weeknight they had to tell me, "a visitation." I asked for every detail, and then promptly locked myself in the bathroom and broke down. I had lost my great-grandmother a couple years before, but I had never experienced a death like this. My dad had struggled with depression and suicidal ideation—a fact to which my own relentless snooping and disregard for boundaries had exposed me at an early age. His dad had also died by suicide, not long after I was born. The concept had been a haunting specter for me previously, but my friend's father's death made it real.

I struggled to place my overwhelming grief. A night or two later, I found myself once again at our church, wandering the halls while my parents attended an event. I ended up in the dark sanctuary. I had gathered in my wanderings the materials for a makeshift altar. At the top of the steps that led to the chancel, in the very center of the open space between the pulpit and lectern and just in front of the Communion table, I laid out my offering. A soft piece of tissue, and on top a beaded cross that I had made, surrounded by dandelions and other weedy flowers I'd found on the church grounds. I'd made the cross with a mix of red beads and white beads with letters that spelled out "I cared."

I left it there in the sanctuary with my tears and my young bewilderment and went home. When Sunday morning came, I returned to the church for worship with my family and found that my grief offering was still there. I was, I think, equal parts shocked, flattered, and embarrassed. It was an ugly little thing. Out of place and awkward, as I so often was in those days. Common sense would have dictated that someone would quietly and gently remove the thing, disposing of it somewhere or maybe tracking down the owner to return it, all before the congregation made its way to Sunday services.

But there it remained. And when the time came, my youth pastor invited all the youngest children of the church to gather on those steps as they did every Sunday for the children's sermon. She pointed out the little altar, and she invited the children to look at it. I think she said something about a God who cares and our call to care for each other. Honestly, I don't remember. What I remember is sitting in my pew and watching this unfold, watching my creation and the grief that propelled it handled with care, respect, and honor. I remember understanding in that moment—with a sort of wondrous and unforgettable certainty that went all the way down to my bones—that I not only belonged in that community, but that I was recognized as someone who added to the church. That the very things that made me different and weird were received as a gift and offering. I suspect I will never forget that feeling. Nor will I forget how rarely in this world our differences are received in such a way.

## Fear, Prejudice, and Normativity
### (How Difference Separates Us)

It's a little sad to me now to think that kids can know that they don't fit in at such an early age. It doesn't take us long, does it? From the day we're born we begin learning about similarity and difference. As toddlers we learn how to tell shapes, colors, letters, and numbers apart from one another. We learn how to match things that are alike. And all the while, we're also being taught that there is right and wrong. A right and a wrong answer. A right and a wrong thing to do. A right and a wrong way to be. At some point, we also learn that "right" equals "normal" and that normal is good. And we learn that "different" is bad or wrong.

Of course, learning to determine the differences and similarities between things isn't inherently a problem. In fact, it's an important part of development. So is learning right from wrong. But this distinction between "normal" and "different" often develops based on majority experience. If *most* people do or think or act a particular way, it becomes normalized.

Problems develop when we construct social and cultural hierarchies and barriers based on normativity, which turn realities of difference into justifications for fear, prejudice, and discrimination. While difference itself is natural, it becomes divisive when we assign value to differences that are inherent. It's one thing to say that people have a different race or a different ethnicity. It is, of course, another thing entirely when we say that one of those races or ethnicities is the norm, and moreover that the "normal" one is good, while the others are bad. We have obviously seen this play out in history in horrific ways, and it is still at play in horrific ways today.

This system of privileging certain identities and characteristics as normative, and therefore better, applies to gender, class, sexuality, place of origin, type of family, intelligence, ability, and on and on. We have woven value hierarchies based on normativity so intricately into our society that we barely notice how deep it goes. And the more "normal" we are, the less likely we are to notice. There are normal and abnormal hobbies, normal and abnormal ways to feel about a popular thing or person, normal and abnormal life timelines. If you like soccer, love Brad Pitt, and get married and have kids, you're normal and that's good. If you like rock collecting, think Brad Pitt is ugly, and never have a relationship at all, you're not just different—you're weird. And weird carries with it a cost, in social capital at least. Obviously, these ways of being outside the norm carry less of a cost than some of the other types of difference named (like race, gender, etc.), because not only have we added value hierarchies to normalcy, we've also added a value hierarchy to types of difference.

The issue separating us here isn't that we recognize or acknowledge difference. The goal certainly isn't erasing differences or imposing sameness. This isn't about "everyone on the soccer team gets a trophy." This is about asking why we're giving metaphorical trophies for things like being white, or male, or American—or for that matter, for liking the right things or people. More deeply, the issue is that we not only value conformity and normativity and dislike difference. We *fear* difference. And in our fear, we cast out those who are different; we deny them place, belonging, safety, and sometimes equity and justice.

When someone is different from us in a way that means we cannot easily relate to them or their experience, we distance ourselves from them and circle the wagons around those whom we consider the same as us. This is especially true for those of us whose qualities and characteristics are deemed most normal and good, and who rely on that system of value for security. Acknowledging that others are different requires us to either label them as "less than" or confront the possibility that some of our value and power is undeserved. We attempt to justify our fear by demonizing those who are different. We transform our fear into hate. And then hate, too, becomes normalized.

There's another thing worth pointing out about assigning value to normativity. When we base our standards of normativity on majority or dominant experience, we expect those with other needs to either adapt or be excluded. Even at our best, we often treat differing needs as a burden or hurdle to be overcome, rather than simply . . . a difference. This bars some people—especially those with differing abilities—from full participation in community, and in their absence, ideas of what is majority experience or normative get further entrenched because they aren't there to challenge the dominant narrative. It's worth asking whether normativity is really more myth than actual functional reality. And even if it's not, it's worth asking: is normal really better?

## "God's People" and God as "They"
### (Difference in the Bible)

An honest look at Scripture reveals that much of the Bible is as likely to reinforce the idea that differences are bad as to reject such a narrative. The story of the ancient Israelites depicted in the Hebrew Testament is one of a people set apart, specially anointed, protected, and loved by God. Many of their countless laws served to protect and highlight their cultural distinctiveness as a people. Non-Israelites, from the Egyptians to the Canaanites to the Moabites and so on, are generally depicted as evil oppressors or sinful idolaters or both. Over and over again, God rains devastation down on those who are not "God's people" while sparing the Israelites with whom God has established an everlasting covenant through Abraham. On the one hand, these ancient stories played a key role in solidifying the identity of the small and often beleaguered nation of Israel. However, some of the biblical stories—in both Testaments—that depict other people as bad or unclean have been used well into the modern era to justify hate and bigotry. For example, the curse of Ham that occurs in Genesis 9 was used by Christians, Muslims, and Jews alike to justify the enslavement and horrific treatment of black people for centuries.

The Tower of Babel in Genesis 11 serves as an etiological myth explaining why the world has different peoples and languages. According to Genesis, at one time all people—who were not so many generations removed from the garden of Eden, and not far removed at all from Noah—were still connected and still spoke one language. They decided to build a mighty tower, determined to make it so tall that it could reach God in heaven. And they worked together to make it happen. Yay for teamwork! Except, God did not appreciate their attempts to match God's might, so God punished them by giving them all different languages so that they couldn't understand each other anymore or coordinate their efforts. Unable to communicate, they abandoned the tower and scattered to the four corners of this world, separated by tongue and identity.

In this story, our differences—some of them anyway—are a punishment from God intended to divide us and break down communication. And we have been divided, it seems, perpetually ever after. Even Jesus, the Son of God himself, showed bias and prejudice. When he encounters the Syrophoenician (or Canaanite) woman who is seeking healing for her daughter, he rejects her, essentially calling her a dog, because she isn't a Jew (Matt. 15:21–28; Mark 7:24–30). Luckily, when she pushes back, he checks himself and praises her faith. This move is one of many during his ministry when Jesus makes it clear that the gospel isn't only for a certain kind of person. But it's also a moment that reminds us of Jesus' humanity, and that he was born into a world defined by difference and judgment.

Despite these instances, the Bible is also chock-full of stories about the acceptability—the holiness, even—of difference, and it starts right at the beginning. In Genesis 1, we're introduced to a God who is described as "they." Verse 26 tells us that God says, "Let us make humankind in our image." Not me. Not mine. God, in this very first chapter of the Bible, is referred to in the plural. Scholars will tell you that the reason for this pronoun trickiness is because when ancient Judaism arose, polytheism was the standard. No one assumed there was only *one* god. Not initially. Down through the years, some Christians have also sought to explain this plurality by claiming that it references the heavenly host—all the angels that serve at God's beck and call. But this plural language also helped early Christians first imagine the Trinity. In the Trinity, and in this origin story, we learn that God contains difference within God's very self, multiple persons distinct yet entwined, somehow both one and three. How can difference be inherently bad, if it's a part of who God is?

The diversity within God's own self is further reflected in what God creates. Countless different animals, plants, land formations, stars, grains of sand. Each its own individual being. Each unique. And all beloved and blessed by God.

And even though Jesus has his moments of prejudice, in Jesus we have a teacher who chooses repeatedly to keep company with those whose differences have made them outcasts in society: those who have disabilities or illnesses, those who are sex workers, children, lepers, tax collectors, and criminals. Jesus sees each person he encounters as worthy of love and care. He preaches that we are to love those who are different from us—even our enemies. In the parable of the Good Samaritan (Luke 10:30–37), Jesus challenges long-held prejudices by making the hero of his story not a rabbi, or even another Jew, but a Samaritan. Of all the people who pass by the man wounded on the side of the road, only the Samaritan stops to help him.

Interestingly, while the Bible makes clear in this story that Samaritans and Jews are not allies, they may not be as different from one another as we think. According to Samaritan tradition, they had been one people until the Babylonian captivity, when the tribes of Judah were exiled. The tribes of Ephraim and Manasseh (Joseph's sons, from whom the Samaritans claim descent) remained behind. While they were separated, their beliefs and traditions evolved in different ways. When the Babylonian exile ended and the two groups faced one another once again, each group thought it had maintained the true faith while the other had strayed. People who had once understood each other came to fear and hate the difference that developed between them.

In the days of Jesus' ministry, Jews and Gentiles were also at odds. Debates raged in the earliest days of the church over what it took to be a follower of Christ. Whether one had to be circumcised, to keep kosher, to follow the letter of the Hebrew law. But Paul preaches an expansive vision of Jesus' church that is big enough to hold different stories, paths, and traditions. In Paul's Letter to the Galatians, he tells us that in Christ "there is no longer Jew or Greek, there is no longer slave or free, there is no longer male and female" (Gal. 3:28). Although many of Paul's words have been used to erect barriers and boundaries in the church that keep some disempowered or excluded entirely, the overarching message of Paul's letters seems to be that what matters is not that we are all the same, but rather that our differences do not determine our worth in the eyes of God.

In his first letter to the people at Corinth, Paul goes even further. In chapter 12, he describes Christ as a body and all of us as those who make up the body of Christ. We are not all the same part, for that would not make a body. Instead, some of us may be an eye or a hand or, heck, even a toenail. And whatever part we are, we can't say to another part, "I have no need of you," nor can anyone say to us, "I have no need of you." The body of Christ needs every part that makes it, and each part has its own unique purpose. In this metaphor, our differences are not only okay, they are crucial—they are the way we effectively and collectively live out God's love in this world.

While the Tower of Babel story paints our different languages and cultures and groups as a punishment instituted by God because of our hubris, Pentecost serves as a powerful witness to the truth that the Holy Spirit is wildly and beautifully at work in our many varied tongues and nations and stories. Through us, through the very things that set us apart and make us distinct from one another, God is at work, connecting us, challenging us, and expanding our understanding of who God is—and who we are.

## The Space between Us
### (How Difference Can Save Us)

In the Trinity, we find the divine gift of difference. The difference and distinction that exist between Creator, Christ, and Spirit also allow God to be in relationship with God's own self. Relationship is inherent to God's very being. God isn't just capable of relationship; God *is* relationship. And that relationship is born out of contrast. Without distinction or difference, there is only one thing, one being. Only endless sameness. But with difference, there is more than one thing, there is contrast, and that allows for relationship to exist between those things that are different. We are created in the image of a God made up of both difference and relationship. And that means we are created for difference, and for the relationship made possible by difference.

Difference isn't what makes us hate each other. Fear does that. Our fear of the unknown, of risk, of what we cannot control because we do not fully understand it. That fear drives us to band together with those we feel connected to by some shared experience or identity. It drives us to push away those who feel too distinct from us. The truth, however, is that we are not exactly the same as *anyone*. We may share the same gender or race or religion or political party. But we are alone in our bodies, in our minds, in our experiences. No two people in this world—no two people who have ever existed or will ever exist—are entirely the same.

We don't have to fear difference. Difference—our own and others'—is how we know who we are. It's how we distinguish ourselves. Our own unique place in this universe and the experiences and qualities that define us allow us to interpret the world around us and make our own particular mark on it. The world is the way it is—different from how it might otherwise have been—because of us. It's also different because of others. The ways that others are different from us, *their* unique experiences and qualities, expose us to new ways to understand the world.

When we choose to connect with others, to love them and get to know them and grow in relationship with them, we are acknowledging that, regardless of whatever similarities we may share, there are ways they are different from us. And we are not only okay with those differences, we are interested in them. Interested in what they hold for us that we cannot find within ourselves. Difference, and the relationships that difference allows us, cultivate growth in us and in others we encounter. We meet each other in our differences, and we each become different, we become *more* than we had been, because of others.

Our theology proposes that God is a supreme being more powerful and infinite than we can imagine. And that means that God is beyond our comprehension. And yet, we also claim that we are created in the image of God, that each human being carries an *imago Dei*. We believe, astoundingly, that who we are reflects something of the truth of who God is. Believing in a God that contains difference within God's own makeup means understanding that we may each carry the image of God in different ways. Recognizing the God-image in others isn't merely a matter of recognizing the ways that we are alike and assuming that those common traits are the marks of God. The very things that make us different from one another may indeed be the marks of God within each of us. In each new person we encounter, each relationship we enter into and cultivate with someone else who also bears the image of God in their own unique way, our understanding of who God is expands. And perhaps we still see through a mirror dimly, as Corinthians tells us—not yet face-to-face with the fullness of who God is—but in relationship, in the embrace of difference and the gifts it offers, we see a little less dimly than before.

In June of 2016, I was working as a pastor at a large downtown church in Chicago. It is an old church, with a long history dating back to the Great Chicago Fire and then some. The church building sits in the heart of the city on a stretch of Michigan Avenue called the Magnificent Mile. I woke up early on the morning of June 12 to arrive at church in time to write an extended Prayers of the People for our 8:00 a.m. worship service, as was the custom. Scrolling through Twitter before I'd even stumbled out of bed, I saw the first comments about a shooting in Orlando, Florida. By the time I'd arrived at church, we knew the site was a nightclub; by the time the first service started, we knew it was a gay nightclub; and by the 11:00 a.m. service, we knew that it was Latinx night at the club, and that the death toll had jumped from around seventeen to fifty, including the shooter. That number made it the worst mass shooting by a single gunman in modern U.S. history, at the time.[2]

From what I gather, that was a horrific morning for many people. A lot of my pastor friends struggled through morning worship as more and more devastating news rolled in. For me, the Pulse nightclub massacre hit particularly hard because, although I am not Latinx or trans, as many of the victims were, I am a member of the LGBTQ community, as many of them were. Just a few hours before the shooting took place, I had been at a queer bar in Chicago with one of my best friends, who is nonbinary and queer, and I'd commented how immediately safe such a space felt compared to the rest of the world. As a relatively young person, in the last moments before the massacre, I had not really known an America where violence on such a scale happened to LGBTQ people.

In the days that followed, I was grateful for the many and varied pockets of community to which I belonged and in which I could seek refuge. That same evening, I was invited to a vigil in my neighborhood, though I chose instead to find comfort in watching the Tony Awards show, aligning myself with the theater community I loved, which also acknowledged and honored the victims of the shooting. That Tuesday I saw a show by my favorite slam poet, Andrea Gibson, a queer and nonbinary person who always speaks raw and beautiful truth in the face of pain. Elsewhere, my circles of LGBTQ and ministry friends checked in on one another from afar. And at the church where I worked, we processed our shock, our horror, and our fear, as well as the theological questions the violent tragedy raised in all of us. I believe that only such a diverse and disparate array of communities allowed me enough space—and spaces—to handle my debilitating grief.

It was my church colleagues' collective response, more than anything else, that signified to me the particular and powerful virtue of difference. On Monday of that week, I learned that churches across the country were being called upon to ring their bells that Wednesday afternoon in honor of the victims. I emailed our head pastor and our music director to ask if we could participate. I was especially timid, in the wake of Orlando, about taking up too much space. I imagined that if they agreed to ring the bells, I would go at that time and stand alone in the courtyard and read the names of each victim aloud, and if they didn't agree to the bells, I'd buy a small one of my own to ring.

I didn't hear back from either my boss or the music director that day, but I arrived to our program staff meeting Tuesday morning to find that not only were they planning to ring the bells, they were already brainstorming how to grow it into something more. I shared that I had planned to read the names in the courtyard, and that quickly became the seed for a prayer service in which we would take turns and each read some of the names. Someone else pointed out that we should do it on the front steps of the sanctuary instead, as a more public witness, and that we should invite community members to join in. Another colleague advocated for involving those we knew from the nearby synagogue and the downtown Islamic center. Yet another minister on our staff suggested that we bring in the band who provided music at our Sunday afternoon jazz service to play at the prayer service. We were lucky to also have the leadership of a Latinx ministry colleague and friend of ours who happened to be in town. We split up the names of the victims, working to learn the proper pronunciations. And then, one of my fellow pastors, whom I'd always known to be relatively quiet and to choose his words carefully, loudly insisted that we buy the largest rainbow flag we could find and hang it above the doors to the sanctuary on Michigan Avenue.

Though my church was justice-oriented and had been more or less supportive of LGBTQ people for many years, it was also large and had many powerful members, and as such, it was extremely careful—frustratingly so, for me—about how it voiced its opinion on "controversial issues." Such a public and bold declaration as a giant rainbow flag over our front doors had never happened before, and would likely never even have been considered had it not been for the horror of Pulse or my colleague's unwavering vehemence. As we sat with this new proposition, the question arose: How long would we leave it up? Just for the day? That felt too brief and dismissive. Just the week? But then Chicago Pride was just after that, and it felt strange to remove it right before Pride. Hanging the flag would no doubt have repercussions. There would be questions, angry phone calls and emails. Were we ready for that? How long could we stand to have the flag hanging, given the drama that would likely unfold?

That question hung in the air, and then our director of business cut in. Typically, it was his role to rein us in, to remind us of potential costs both financial and otherwise, to urge caution. I waited for him to offer the sobering word. But instead he said, "Heck, let's leave it up the whole month!" And we did. The church has hung it up every year since.

That Wednesday afternoon, we gathered on the steps outside our sanctuary with a crowd that spilled out onto Michigan Avenue. Passersby honked at us in support. The giant rainbow flag flapped around in the wind. And we sang and prayed, held hands, read the names, tolled the bell, and wept. What struck me in that moment, and in the staff meeting the previous day when our plans for the prayer service first came together, was how each one of us had something different that we insisted be a part of the service. I only insisted on ringing the bell and reading the names.

But others brought to the table their conviction of who else we involved, and where the service occurred, and what it looked like, and that giant rainbow flag. And only because we were each different—we each brought something different into the process—was the prayer service able to develop into something as powerful and meaningful as it did.

## The "Diversity" Problem

The idea that our differences should be celebrated isn't new. The last few decades, at least, have been marked by a cultural movement to celebrate differences. More often than not, the word used to describe these efforts has been "diversity." America was first celebrated as a melting pot given the many different people, cultures, and histories it contains, and then as a giant salad bowl, in acknowledgment that our differences aren't lost when we become one country. In theory, diversity talk attempts to respond to historic efforts to force assimilation upon those whose differences from those in power has led to their oppression, to discrimination, hatred, and even violence against them. Diversity is intended to reject the idea that sameness and conformity to the norm—and thus the erasure of differences—are ideal or virtuous. It's meant to oppose the belief that some characteristics and identifiers—whiteness, straightness, maleness, and so on— are inherently better than others. But as it has taken root in our cultural conversation, diversity has often been watered down to function in a much less powerful and more banal way.

In a 2015 essay for Salon, sociology professor Ellen Berrey makes the claim that "diversity" has become a code word— language we use to talk about race when we (particularly those of us who are white) don't know *how* to talk about race.[3] Berrey explains that while diversity isn't an inherently bad concept, it becomes problematic when it functions as a means to avoid confronting structural inequalities and systemic discrimination on the basis of race (or, for that matter, gender or sexuality, etc.). She says, "Rather than a righteous fight for justice or effective anti-discrimination laws, we get a celebration of cultural difference as a competitive advantage. Diversity, we are told, is an end goal with instrumental pay-offs: good for learning, good for the bottom line, even good for white people."

Recognizing that differences exist, even saying that they're good, doesn't mean much if we're not willing to recognize the systems and realities that still firmly disadvantage people of a different race or other identifier. When we stop at saying, "We're diverse and we're happy about it," we can't actually move toward a world that embodies that claim. Instead, people of color, or LGBTQ people, or women, or others become tokens that we hold up to prove our appreciation for difference, rather than whole and complex human beings who are part of the fabric of our communities and communities in their own right. Embracing the gift of difference requires us to let go of the ways we've used difference as a weapon and a justification for violence and mistreatment. It requires that we confront our discomfort around tense topics.

Another powerful point that Berrey raises, which I've only alluded to previously, is the damage that comes from flattening all differences to suggest they operate on the same level—which often happens in broad-stroke references to diversity. Assuming all differences are equal fools us into believing that unity is just a matter of acknowledging that difference exists and that it isn't inherently bad, without doing any work to recognize systemic inequalities rooted in difference. It allows us to believe that every type of difference can coexist without any profound shift in our power structures or any pursuit of transformative justice. Difference is everywhere in our world, but we've used some differences to enslave, eradicate, violate, and dehumanize people. These differences and the oppression we've justified on their basis require a level of reckoning and deconstruction that other differences don't. Claims of unity in diversity that don't confront the very real ongoing disparities our society justifies on the basis of difference are hollow and dangerous. Honest conversations about how difference has functioned to separate and divide us require us to recognize these disparities in impact and value, and work to overcome them, before any true diversity or unity can exist.

## What Do We Do with Difference?

We've established that differences, while they can be a cause for fear and prejudice, are also a gift that allows relationship to grow. At the same time, embracing the gifts of difference requires us to ask hard questions about why and how we celebrate diversity, and for whom. This doesn't mean that we become afraid again of difference or afraid of celebrating difference wrongly. It only means that we must be intentional and discerning about honoring well the various ways we are different. In short, we must work at it. So, what does this look like in practice?

Even in communities built around commonalities (perhaps especially in these spaces), some needs and perspectives are privileged over others. We embrace the gifts of difference when we are discerning about what differences of experience, need, and perspective are going unrecognized, and seek to consider them alongside whatever has been deemed "normative."

Part of this work requires us to also acknowledge that not all breaks from whatever is considered "the norm" carry the same weight or have the same consequence in our society. Some differences—like marital status or athletic ability—may cause someone to be left out or feel unseen or unaccepted by their communities. And the pain that may cause a person is real and worthy of acknowledgment. But other differences—whether gender, race, sexuality, class, or ability, to name a few—have been the basis for immense mistreatment and injustice, with impacts that last generations and reach into every pocket of our society. The magnitude of this fearful reaction to difference must be seen and understood before we can move to a place of truly honoring the ways that we are all different.

Embracing the gifts of difference calls upon us to allow those differences to impact us and the communities we create, and to understand how they already have impacted us and our communities. It's not enough to simply see difference and say that it is good. It's not enough to welcome those who are different—whether by identity or experience or otherwise—into our communities. Embracing difference isn't about grafting new people onto our communities like Dr. Frankenstein stitching a new arm onto his monster. The true gift and challenge are that we understand that people different from us are *already* a part of our collective community. And where we've prevented that by erecting barriers, we can't simply open a door to let in folks we've excluded. Our communities must be shaped as much by their experiences and identities as by our own. A community truly made up of diverse people and realities is a community shaped by all the stories it contains, and it becomes, by virtue of difference, more than the sum of its parts.

When we judge, reject, oppress, and mistreat other people on the basis of inherent differences—when we allow those differences to justify our hating others or treating them as less beloved by God than us, as less than human—we are not just rejecting them. We are rejecting the God-image in them. Too often in these angry and polarized days, we give ourselves permission to reject the God-image in others. Sometimes this rejection happens as a matter of discrimination and bigotry, and other times it comes from a place of righteous rage over injustices that have occurred. These reasons are not equivalent, and it's dangerous to treat them equally. But somehow, we must find our way to a place where we remember and acknowledge that every person bears the image of God and is loved by God. Wherever that distant place is, God is waiting for us, holding the hope for a better world.

*Chapter Two*

# The Gift of Doubt

Sitting next to my seminary classmate Gordon in the fall of 2011, I nursed a beer and shifted nervously on my creaky bar stool at the Local Pub and Patio in Austin, Texas. That dive bar would be the primary hangout for me and most of my friends for the rest of our grad school careers, bearing witness to as many of my late-night cram sessions, paper-writing marathons, and rowdy theological debates as any building on campus. But on this night, only a month or so into school, it was still new and unfamiliar, just like everything else about seminary had turned out to be.

I was twenty-five, tall and freckled, both eager and brimming with a little too much ego in my newfound academic sweet spot. I swaggered into seminary with all the self-assuredness of anyone who'd grown up spending as much time in church as out, memorizing Scripture verses on index cards, sweeping every Bible category on *Jeopardy!* by age eleven, and writing praise songs to Jesus on the back of my worship bulletins. And though I did well in my classes, I, like most anyone else who shows up to earn a master of divinity degree in such a state of unyielding certainty, quickly ran smack-dab into an utter upheaval of faith.

That evening at the bar I was in good company. Gordon was a middle-aged former lawyer from Louisiana, and he had been running up against his own frustrations and questions as our Old Testament and theology classes shook the foundations of his

Christian understanding. After a lifetime of Sunday school classes and Bible studies, we were now learning about how our sacred text was pieced together from various murky sources, as well as other religions, and how many scholars believe that the God of Eden is not the same God that Moses encounters in the burning bush. Our theology class, meanwhile, was challenging us to consider the idea that all of our language about God was merely a flawed and limited attempt to describe that which we could never really understand.

So, Gordon and I sat there, sipping beer and empathizing with one another, reminding each other that this was all part of the calling. After a little while, he leaned in toward me conspiratorially and said with a smile and his gentle southern drawl, "You know, Anne Lamott says, 'The opposite of faith isn't doubt, it's certainty.'"

Seminarians are not, of course, the only Christians bumping into doubts about their faith. Messy faith perspectives like that epitomized in Lamott's writing have gained increasing traction in popular Christianity in recent decades. Many have found solace in the notion that doubt itself is not a failure of faith, and might rather be a natural component of Christian life.

Still, doubt has dangerous potential to create rifts between people and—especially, perhaps—within faith communities. Doubt raises questions. And questions introduce the possibility that what has been accepted as truth might, in fact, be wrong. What if the previously always-accepted answer turns out to be wrong—or just not the only right answer? Doubt in authority figures undermines their power and the trust their followers have in them. Doubt in shared beliefs or purpose or methodology can threaten the cohesion of a group, which, of course, threatens the unity of said group. What if doubt leads one to discover that they and those they love most do not share the same crucial convictions? Doubt can send us on journeys that lead us toward new truths and away from the path that others walk, and if the goal is that we all walk the same way, then doubt is danger. The solution, then, is to forbid doubt, or else sanitize it and allow it in only acceptable and incremental ways. So often, for the unity we've created to persist, any doubt about that which binds us together, be it belief, system, or person, must be avoided at all costs.

## Doubt and Drawing Near
### (Doubt in the Bible)

No biblical figure is more thoroughly associated with doubt than Thomas, whose postresurrection dubiousness and resultant rebuke from Jesus earned him an immortalized nickname, Doubting Thomas. Of course, Thomas was also the disciple with the faith to proclaim, "Let us also go, that we may die with him," in the face of Jesus' execution (John 11:16). But that statement of total devotion has been largely eclipsed by his later skepticism. Whatever else Thomas might have been, we know him now only as the twin of an unknown sibling, and the one who doubted.

As the story in the Gospel of John goes, Jesus has died painfully and publicly on the cross, been buried, and then, remarkably, vanished from the tomb in which he was laid. Since that disappearance, he has reappeared twice. First to Mary as she wept by the empty tomb, and then to almost all of the disciples inside the room in which they have locked themselves out of fear. Indeed, this visit from the resurrected Christ occurs just before Thomas arrives, in what has to be one of the worst cases of bad timing ever.

He shows up from wherever he'd been and is suddenly swamped by his amazed fellow Christ-followers who tell him about the encounter that has just occurred. Thomas is skeptical and says as much.

When Jesus shows up again a week later, he lets Thomas touch his wounds, and then commends the faith of those who, unlike Thomas, believe without seeing. Honestly, it's a bit of an awkward whiplash from the intimate moment of physical reunion to the parental chastising. I feel for Thomas. Granted, what the other disciples describe to Thomas—that is, Jesus returned to life—is something he'd been told to expect by Jesus himself. Still, Thomas essentially asks for what the other disciples have already been given. They've had the privilege of seeing for themselves. Who's to say that any one of them would have been any less skeptical?

Thomas has long represented a cautionary tale for believers about the shortcomings of doubt. But many of the pastors I know these days relish the chance to preach on this passage, not so they can spell out the sinfulness of Thomas's doubt, but rather to highlight how relatable he is.

As Frederick Buechner once preached, "It's hard to imagine that there's a believer anywhere who wouldn't have traded places with Thomas, given the chance, and seen that face and heard that voice and touched those ruined hands."[1]

And it seems all the more fitting that this text is most often preached shortly after Easter Sunday, when all the hallelujahs and declarations that "he is risen indeed!" have already given way to the day-to-day struggles to maintain faith in God in a world that is very much still broken. In Thomas, we see some hope for ourselves. If even one of the Twelve can doubt, then surely we are not doomed for doing the same.

While Thomas may have the nickname, Peter has his moments of doubt too. And never is his doubt more apparent than when Jesus walks on water (Matt. 14:22–33). Matthew, Mark, and John all contain accounts of this pivotal miracle, and in each of them the event occurs just after Jesus has miraculously multiplied a scant few loaves and fishes into an abundance for more than five thousand. Only Matthew turns his attention to Peter and his overzealous antics. After the thousands have been adequately fed, and the leftovers gathered, Jesus urges the disciples to take off in the boat and head to the other side of the lake. He stays behind to disperse the crowds, and then disappears to pray on top of a mountain. When he returns, he finds that his friends in the boat are being beaten up by rough waves and sets out on foot, walking on top of the water to reach them.

Though the specifics vary, the Gospel writers are consistent, and understandably so, that this nonchalant miracle freaks the bejeezus out of the disciples. Among them, only Peter responds by upping the ante. While the others cower and try to recover their wits, Peter tells Jesus that if it is really him, he should command that Peter get out of the boat and walk over to him. And Jesus, ever the bluff-caller, says, "Come." To Peter's credit, he does get out of the boat and he's fine for a bit until a strong gust of wind reminds him of the ridiculousness of the situation. Then he wavers and begins to sink, crying out to Jesus for help.

Thomas and Peter are different from one another. And it's worth noting that the word "doubt" never actually comes up in Thomas's story. It appears only in Peter's story, when Jesus asks him, "You of little faith, why did you doubt?" Still, given that his doubts are almost all we know about Thomas, we're left with an impression of him as a constant questioner, a pathological needer of proof. Peter, for his part, seems to vacillate wildly between zealous, unexamined faith and endless uncertainty. What the two men doubt differs too. Though ultimately both are questioning the extent of Jesus' power, Thomas's doubts are primarily about what Jesus is capable of, while Peter's doubts—at least in this instance—are about what his faith in Christ gives him the power to do. I suspect none of us are strangers to either kind of doubt if we have a well-examined faith.

The most compelling instance of doubt in the Bible, in my opinion, comes from the Son of God himself. In the Garden of Gethsemane, Jesus trembles and falls to his knees. He prays and begs for the company of his friends. He asks that there be some way that this future he faces—this torture and death—be taken from him (Matt. 26:39; Luke 22:42). And though he follows this request with a reassertion of his commitment to God's will, he does not recant his desperate request.

And then, when he has been betrayed, arrested, flogged and humiliated, nailed to a cross, and left to die a slow and excruciating death, strung up between two criminals, he cries out to God. "Eloi, Eloi, lema sabachthani?" (Matt. 27:46; Mark 15:34; quoting Ps. 22:1).

"My God, my God, why have you forsaken me?"

Though many try, it is hard to spin this moment as anything other than abject despair, a genuine sense of abandonment, and bitter doubt on the part of Jesus. It is a devastating moment. But it is also a moment, for all its darkness, weighty with the promise of grace unlike any other single moment in our Scriptures. Though we most venerate Jesus' bold confrontation with and overthrow of death, it is his moment of doubt that offers us a salve for our own struggles. In this lifetime, we cannot know the feeling of death. But for those of us whose hope rests in God, the moments when we genuinely doubt God's love for us or God's very existence feel lonely and Godforsaken like nothing else. And in this moment on the cross, Jesus enters into that hopeless place—and meets us there. In a moment of perfect vulnerability, he exemplifies the very heart of humanness and assures us that even in our doubts about God, we are not alone.

Surely, if the one who is without sin knows the pain of doubt, then we cannot ourselves be considered sinful for doubting too.

## Be It Dogma, Methodology, or Unity Itself
### (How Doubt Separates Us)

Despite the comfort we may take from Jesus' solidarity with us in our doubts, both the existence of doubt and our postures toward it have done much to separate us from one another. Culturally, we face daily news stories about scandal and immorality that force us to doubt the goodness and trustworthiness of our leaders and those who put them in power. Meanwhile, we throw barbs of betrayal at anyone who openly names such doubts, and in our ever-spiraling dialogue come to doubt the goodwill, the intelligence, and even, at times, the humanity of one another. Accusations of fake news and conspiracies undermine our trust in any reliable source of truth, and we are left with nothing but our questions and our anger at those who took away our ability to feel certain.

In the church, doubt is even more loaded. In fundamentalist churches, the Bible is believed to have been written by God through its human authors and thus to be without flaw. To question any part of it is to question God, and to question God in this understanding of Christian faith is to sin. In an essay published on John Piper's Desiring God website, Greg Morse bemoans the sinfulness of doubt, saying, "the Holy Spirit in us never protects or encourages doubt," and that "being content with doubt, suspicion, and weak faith is, as Luther says, the highest form of contempt we can muster against God."² For Morse, believing that our questions are anything less than an insult to God is to betray our faith.

Even in those conservative churches where intellectual exploration and questions are welcomed, there remains an expectation that you ultimately arrive at the same tried-and-true theological answers and biblical interpretations. In these cases, the questioning that is allowed functions as a sort of intellectual or spiritual rumspringa. If one dares to push beyond the limits of those sanctioned questions, or perhaps is unwilling to eventually relinquish one's doubts, one faces at best rebuke and at worst wholesale and lasting rejection.

It does not seem to matter much that there are contradictions within the biblical text itself. Nor that interpretations even within conservative and traditionalist circles have evolved over time. Attempts to persuade biblical literalists or traditionalists by pointing to the variety of Old Testament definitions of marriage, for example, or by highlighting hypocrisies in modern faith practice (for example, that straight Christians get divorced, don't separate their meat and dairy, and don't make women cover their heads) are generally dismissed as hyperbolic and thus irrelevant. What matters is unwavering faith in the Bible *as it is understood to be* (and supposedly always has always been) by those in leadership, and a fierce hostility toward doubt of biblical teachings, a doubt that is to be avoided or, if necessary, overcome.

In theory, progressive churches should offer an ideal alternative. They generally concede that the Bible was written by human beings, who were flawed and bound by the biases and limitations of their context. Given this, such subsets of modern Christianity tend to base their rejection of the idea that homosexuality is sinful on the premise that modern constructs of consensual love and same-sex relationships didn't exist in any significant way in biblical times. Passages that declare that women should be silent or that divorce is adultery are recognized as speaking to a particular demographic at a particular time. Other passages are quietly avoided as fairly irredeemable (psalms about bashing babies' heads in, for example, or the story about the bears devouring children). Paul, with all his thorn-in-the-flesh sexual repression, is held in equal parts esteem and exasperation.

In these circles, doubts around biblical interpretation are not only accepted, they're expected. But doubt still has a destructive role to play in these iterations of Christianity. For progressive Christians, doubt becomes a problem when people question what constitutes justice and what methodology should be employed to achieve it. In a 2018 article about US politics for the Australian Broadcasting Corporation's Religion and Ethics website, titled "Why the Religious Left Is a Political Failure," leftist Christian writer Daniel José Camacho points out, "Accounts of the religious left typically blur any distinction between theological liberalism and progressive politics. The two are not synonymous. In other words, one can approach the bible critically, revise traditional dogma and strive for an inclusive church while subscribing to a number of policies and political agendas."[3]

As Camacho suggests, there is little room within the "religious left"—at least as it is understood institutionally—for people whose views are still evolving or who align with the progressive movement in most, but not all, ways. The institution of progressive Christianity may admit the ways that it is still racist, sexist, heterosexist, and far short of fully living out the justice ideals it proclaims, but it resists genuine analysis of its structural integrity in this regard and balks at any doubts raised about whether it may be, by its institutional nature, inherently and irredeemably problematic.

Then there is the moderate middle. This portion of the modern church is generally made up of "purple congregations"—a newly popular term to describe congregations that contain a diversity of political perspectives. The moderate middle is also occupied by individuals who either don't share strong convictions about the issues that define others as conservative and progressive, or simply have much stronger convictions about the danger of division. For these folks, doubts over both tradition and modern justice movements are welcome to a point. In fact, a certain degree of skepticism toward both is expected. What the moderate middle does not allow is utter certainty about the rightness of one's own position nor a belief that one's position is worth maintaining even if it leaves some people behind. In the moderate middle, unity reigns supreme, and doubting its ultimate importance is seen as selfishness, arrogance, or ignorance.

This subset has made itself known repeatedly in denominational debates over human sexuality. In 2014, in the months leading up to the Presbyterian Church (U.S.A.)'s national denominational gathering—General Assembly—the faculty of both Columbia Theological Seminary and Austin Presbyterian Theological Seminary issued a letter to the voting commissioners urging unity above all.[4] There were two pivotal votes on the church's stance on LGBTQ marriage equality coming before the Assembly, as well as another controversial vote on whether to divest from three American companies working in Israel. The Austin Seminary letter called for "mutual forbearance" in the face of these divisive issues and suggested that "perhaps the one thing worse than those in disagreement sitting on the same pew is those in disagreement NOT sitting on the same pew." While this particular letter and many who find themselves in this middle space seem comfortable with dialogue and even argument, they leave no space to doubt or question whether unity—staying together—is more important than anything else.

In all of these instances, doubt drives a wedge between people of faith. However, in most cases, it's fear of what doubt *could* do rather than the doubts themselves that creates the uncrossable line. For conservatives, there is risk in allowing people to question what the church teaches, and the risk is theological divergence. The risk is finding out that what you've always thought you believed may no longer be what you, or others you love, believe. For progressives, the risk in letting others doubt the institution, the specific tenets, and the methodology of progressive Christianity's justice orientation is being forced to confront inherent, overlooked flaws and fractures within the broader community. And for moderates, the risk in embracing those who doubt unity as the absolute goal, of course, is division. These fears are valid because the potential consequences of doubt are real. The question, though, is, are these consequences all that bad? Are they worse than what is allowed to fester when doubt is treated as sin? What if, in setting our fears of doubt aside, we found that doubt itself can be not just acceptable, but an important gift?

### Beauty Secrets from a Snake
### (A Case Study in Doubt's Benefits)

For all that it runs contrary to our traditional understanding of faith, doubt ultimately has the power to help us grow in depth of faith by allowing us to deeply examine what we've been taught and discover what we actually believe.

All those years ago at that bar in Austin, my classmate Gordon and I shared the common struggle of doubt and faith upheaval. I'd grown up learning to ask questions and wrestle with the uncertainties of faith. I had been well warned that seminary is a place where people either embrace questions or find their faith destroyed by them. Most of what we'd learned in class energized and fascinated me, spoke to me so deeply and naturally that it was as if it were in a language I'd never realized I already knew. I was mostly ready for doubts about the teachings of my conservative Christian upbringing. Or at least, I thought I was. What I wasn't prepared for was the sudden reckoning with doubt over how much longer I could go on without confronting the truth that I was queer.

After more than a decade of avoiding too close an examination of my sexuality, just two weeks into seminary, both my classes and my personal life were finally forcing me to confront the question. In classes, we were being taught that to be created in the image of an inherently relational (that is, Trinitarian) God is to have authentic relationship—with God, others, and ourselves—as our highest calling and that authentic relationship requires honesty with ourselves and others about our vulnerabilities and who we are. In my personal life, I was suddenly surrounded, for the first time, by classmates who were openly queer and pursuing not only lives of faith, but lives of ministry. I was also falling in love with my classmate Molly.

While I have no explicit memory of being taught in church that homosexuality was wrong, I certainly got the message. At first, in my early teens, I determined that actions mattered more than feelings. And I decided that if I ever realized I might not be straight, I would refuse to act on that realization. Over the years, as I realized I knew and loved people who were gay, lesbian, and bisexual, I rejected that theology and believed that those who were gay and bisexual and trans were beloved by God exactly as they were. I thought I was certain. I thought that my questions around that theology had been dealt with. But when I could no longer avoid the truth that I myself was queer, I was suddenly flooded with doubts and questions again. In my own denomination, LGBTQ ordination had been approved just months earlier,[5] and it was still causing major conflict.

I know what it is to be afraid of doubts. Because back in those early days of seminary, I was terrified of my doubts. Terrified of my doubts about my own beliefs. Terrified of my doubts about my sexuality. Terrified of my doubts about my own strength to own my identity and face an uncertain future.

And in the midst of all that fear, uncertainty, doubt, and reckoning, the professors who taught my Colloquy on Vocation and Ministry class assigned us to find a spot to be alone and commune with some piece of nature for an hour while listening to our thoughts and the Holy Spirit. Let me tell you, in those days there was nothing I wanted less than an hour alone with my thoughts. My thoughts had become weapons that I feared would shatter my life.

Grumbling, I resolved to sit in my favorite place on our seminary campus: a storm drain right next to a wooden footbridge, looking out over the creek that divided our campus in two. I decided I would find a squirrel to commune with. Squirrels seemed safe and distracting. A minute or two after I had settled into my spot, I heard telltale rustling on the opposite bank and searched for the squirrel I assumed was responsible for the noise.

But it wasn't a squirrel. Out from the crunchy leaves and under-growth, a long black snake appeared.

It's important at this point in the story to know that snakes rank somewhere in the top five of my greatest fears, and so before my brain had even fully registered what was happening, I was on my feet and ready to run to the closest shelter and lock the door. But because I was a first-year seminarian and thus believed that every moment of life was brimming with spiritual significance, I thought that perhaps this snake too had something to teach me. I forced myself to sit back down and wait and watch. I watched as the snake slithered down the bank slowly. I watched as it soaked up the sun on its black scales. I watched as it caught and ate a frog.

Suddenly I was weeping. I thought about how so much of my fear and hatred of snakes came from a narrative that I had inherited and learned, both from the culture around me and especially from Christianity. I thought about how false and destructive that seemed, watching this creature go about life. I realized that this snake, like any other thing, was a beloved creation of God, knit together intricately in love.

I thought about myself and how I knew—had known for a long time, deep down—that I was queer. And I began to question the narratives of fear and hate that I had inherited from my religion. I realized that underneath my doubts about my own goodness and God-belovedness was a deeper certainty that I was fearfully and wonderfully made, just as the psalmist says, and just as this creature sharing the creek bank with me was. I had been overcome with doubt about whether I was strong enough to come out, whether my family would still love me, whether I could still be a minister, whether I could still be Christian. But when I confronted those doubts on that autumn afternoon, I found that I could meet each of them with a new question: What if I am strong enough? What if they do still love me? What if I can still be a minister? And what if I already was both queer and Christian?

I had been running from my truth for so long because I was terrified of the doubts it would require me to confront. But weeping in the middle of my Texas seminary while I communed with God and a snake, I stood face-to-face with my doubts, and they led me to discover a deeper faith than I have ever known. In the absence of rigid certainty, my doubts allowed hope to blossom and created possibility for a different and better understanding of God. In facing my doubts over whether I could ever be good enough or right enough or straight enough for God to love me, I discovered a new knowing that God already did love me, that I was already good exactly as I was.

I was far from ready to come out to my family, even after that life-changing encounter by the creek, but I was so on fire from the experience that I couldn't keep entirely silent about it. And so, the very next night, I wrote an entry on my blog—the only devoted reader of which, I'm pretty sure, was my mom—and described the entire encounter and what it had taught me about questioning narratives of demonization and learning to embrace who God created us to be, avoiding any specific mention of who God created *me* to be.

When I nervously asked my mom several days later if she'd read it, she responded, "Yes, and I've been meaning to reply, but I wanted to talk to you about it over the phone." I was, of course, terrified all over again. Had she figured the whole thing out?

When she called me, however, what she shared was both remarkable and completely unexpected. She told me that she had read my blog post first thing in the morning when she woke up. The night before, she'd had a dream. And in the dream, someone—she couldn't see who—was trying to force her to hold a snake. She didn't want to hold it, and she was afraid, but she didn't have a choice. So, she held the snake, and she still didn't really want to, but she realized she was okay, that there was nothing to be afraid of.

After that, she woke up and read my blog about my encounter with a snake by the creek. "Isn't that so totally weird?" she asked me. "Wow," I said, "yeah," feeling strangely comforted.

Sometimes, embracing doubt means learning that you have nothing to be afraid of. Sometimes it means doing unimaginably hard things. And sometimes, it means discovering truth and hope that you can't imagine having gone the entire rest of your life without.

## Doubt as a Gift
## (How Doubt Can Save Us)

Though the Bible gives them a hard time, Thomas and Peter and the others who encounter doubt find gifts in the process as well. Thomas admits that he won't believe that Jesus is truly returned to human life until he touches the wounds on his hands and in his side. In so doing, he names the fear and doubt that frankly all the disciples have been exhibiting since Jesus was first arrested, and thus opens a way to another encounter with Christ and a conversation about those very doubts. Note too that while the disciples who had the privilege of being present when Jesus first appeared in the locked room apparently only saw Jesus' wounds with their eyes, Thomas is invited to touch Jesus and to touch the places where he hurts. Jesus offers praise for those who will believe without needing to see or touch—because of course there will be many such. Nevertheless, Thomas's doubts draw him into closer, tangible relationship with Christ and, ultimately, deeper knowing.

Peter fares similarly. Remember that it is his doubt about Jesus suddenly appearing that compels him to climb out of the boat. Indeed, his doubt and his desire for deeper knowing draw him, miraculously, across the water. His doubt also causes him to sink, apparently, but not before it has drawn him close enough to Jesus for the Messiah to reach down and give him a hand. And Jesus, while we'll never know quite what happened between him and God, found in voicing his doubt both a deeper closeness with humanity and the strength to face his fate.

There's no use pretending that doubt is entirely good. Certainly, when we only ever doubt each other, we find it difficult if not impossible to establish trust. When we only ever question ourselves, we struggle to find the self-confidence to move forward or stand in our full truth. When all we have is doubt, it's hard to find our way to hope.

My confrontation with doubts around my theology, my identity, and my relationships had real and terrible cost. I confronted doubts about what I had been taught, and I had to leave the church I'd grown up in (though we reconciled, in the end). I faced and continue to face those who question my credibility as a minister because I doubt oppressive traditional interpretations of theology and Scripture. Confronting my doubts about being able to avoid my queerness meant, in many ways, walking a different and separate and sometimes even opposed path from those I love. And coming out—facing all of those doubts and questions about what I understood even about my progressivism—has forced me to reckon repeatedly with my own biases, my privilege, my prejudice, and my shortcomings of thought.

Still, doubt has gifts to offer. Doubting the beliefs I'd been taught also unshackled me from a theology of self-loathing. It allowed me to embrace my religion and my God-given identity and find my calling at their meeting place. It deepened the authenticity of my relationships with those I loved, even if it has also made them more difficult in certain ways. It has made me a better activist, a better pastor, and a better Christian. I have discovered myself, and God, in new ways.

What if we allowed people to doubt and question and challenge beliefs? What if, because of this, we had a more robust faith collectively? What if we listened to folks who challenged our methods, structures, and priorities? What if we joined with them in the work, or even worked separately with shared commitments, and saw greater progress toward justice and more integrity because of it? What if we let people doubt unity as the unassailable objective? What if we let people fight it out and separate and walk different paths—for a bit or for a lifetime—recognizing that we still belong to one another by God's love and that we are bound for the same destination? What if we engaged with doubt, neither as lying trickster nor arbiter of truth, but as an invitation toward growth?

Being human requires reckoning with doubt. As long as our minds are capable of critical thought, we will come face-to-face with it. To pretend that it doesn't exist, to try to erase it or ignore it, will only tire us out, while doubt looms as large as ever—a wall or barrier to one another, to God, and to understanding. Doubt, when confronted and even embraced, offers a doorway to discovery. And on the other side? Perhaps we find ourselves that much closer to one another, to God, to truth. Or at least, with a much better view.

# Chapter Three

# The Gift of Argument

Disney's 1950 animated version of *Cinderella* portrays the "evil stepmother" as a tall, stiff-backed, sneering woman in high collars, with graying hair pulled back in a regal bun, who stares down her nose at Cinderella and anyone else she deems beneath her. The stepmother, Lady Tremaine, makes demands of her stepdaughter in a haughty voice that carries a trace of sickening glee, and whenever Cinderella protests or attempts to argue, the stepmother throws out her hand, index finger pointed sharply toward Cinderella, and barks, "Silence!"

I grew up in a fairly strict and disciplined household. It was, of course, nothing at all like Cinderella's, but as a child I *felt* as though I was constantly getting reprimanded. I did not take well to discipline. As a very young child, I was constantly testing the limits and pushing back, and then when I inevitably got into trouble for my behavior, I would cry and scream at the injustice of it all. I hated getting punished, but apparently not enough to stay out of trouble.

Instead, around age four or five, I took a page from Lady Tremaine's book. Whenever I had done something wrong and gotten caught or pushed limits too far, and I could tell that an adult was about to scold me, I would throw out my hand, point a finger sharply toward the adult, and say in the firmest voice I could, "Silence!" I'll admit, it was not my most effective strategy. But

I was convinced that if I could just keep them from speaking, I could avoid any heartache or conflict or consequences. My mom will tell you that it was hard not to laugh whenever I did my "silence!" move, but she restrained herself.

Despite my sometimes insolent early childhood behavior, growing up in the South instilled in me a thorough education on the value of silence and the impropriety of disagreement. In the South, politeness is a way of life. We are taught to say "yes, ma'am" and "no, sir" and when not to speak at all. We're taught to swallow our anger and hold our tongues rather than speak out of turn or incite conflict. We learn early on that some topics are "not fit for polite company" and some family stories are best left untold. Argument is to be avoided at all costs, especially when there is a power differential or when the topic is heated and controversial. When disagreements occur, they must always be measured, restrained, and well mannered. Argument—which in my mind often carries with it a passionate tone and necessary but sometimes brutal honesty—defied social norms of "polite disagreement." Above all, we are made to understand that talking back is profoundly disobedient and disrespectful, and should not be tolerated.

Of course, this structure of conflict avoidance is not particular to the American South. Over the years, I've heard similar stories from friends who grew up in the Midwest and particularly from friends who come from immigrant families. In her book *Everything I Never Told You*, Celeste Ng tells the story of a biracial Chinese American family who lose their middle daughter in a tragic drowning but are unable to fully understand what happened to her and why because they are each keeping secrets from the others out of love and obedience—secrets that obscure the truth of the girl's death and impede any peace that may come from a fuller understanding.

Describing how the youngest child learns the crucial role of her silence in her family's life, Ng writes, "Hannah, as if she understood her place in the cosmos, grew from quiet infant to watchful child: a child fond of nooks and corners, who curled up in closets, behind sofas, under dangling tablecloths, staying out of sight as well as out of mind, to ensure the terrain of the family did not change."[1]

Though particularly potent in the family of Ng's novel, this fear of conflict, upheaval, and argument undergirds much of our culture and social history. The risk of speaking up, of arguing against, of taking a contrary position and being honest and passionate about it is that you bring shame to your family and your community, and in so doing destroy relationships. This fear is also at the heart of the modern Christian church. While some traditions, like my own Presbyterian denomination, encourage questions and understand that people of good faith can disagree, there are still deeply entrenched expectations of how we disagree and when and how intensely. We employ complex systems, rules, and procedures for how to engage civilly even in our disagreement rather than devolve into "needlessly hostile argument." Failure to comply with these expectations is perceived as a threat to the unity of the church and even, at times, disobedience to God.

## Obedience versus Argument in the Bible

Obedience is a consistent theme throughout the biblical text. Those claiming its significance in the life of faith will find no shortage of support for their conviction. The very first human story in Genesis is arguably one of a failure to obey and the consequences that arise from that disobedience. God gives Adam and Eve the freedom to name and care for all creatures in existence, to enjoy the abundant fruits and pleasures of Eden, and to live a life unhampered by shame and fear. But God also gives them a single boundary. One rule: Do not eat the fruit from the tree of the knowledge of good and evil. God warns Adam, "in the day that you eat of it you shall die" (Gen. 2:17).

In Adam and Eve's defense, they seem pretty committed to following this rule, right up until the serpent comes along. Eve, having not yet eaten from the tree of the knowledge of good and evil, has no reason or even capacity to suspect the serpent of ill will. For the first time in her existence, someone has offered her an alternative to God's command. He tells her that eating from the tree won't kill her after all. In essence, the serpent has presented a counterargument to God: the possibility that there is more to the truth than what Eve already knows. And she's intrigued. Honestly, I don't think it's entirely fair to expect her to know that something is wrong—even disobedience. She literally doesn't understand good and evil precisely *because* she hasn't eaten from the tree.

The serpent also isn't wrong. Eve and Adam eat the fruit, it's delicious, and afterward they do not—in fact—die. They just realize that they're naked and that some things are right and some are wrong and they have, apparently, just done the latter. Being perpetually disinclined toward obedience myself, I feel a fair amount of sympathy for these two bumbling humans. Still, there's no denying that given the choice between God's command and the serpent's intriguing alternative, Eve (and Adam) hardly hesitate before setting God's instructions aside in favor of another path. This disobedience supposedly enacts a chain of events that lead to the utter fall of humanity, at least according to modern Christian understanding.

From Abraham's covenant to Moses' ten commandments, David's kingship, and even Jesus' own teachings and life and death and resurrection—the Bible is almost entirely a book of God making promises to humanity on the singular condition that humanity obey God's commands, and humanity subsequently messing it up. Ours is mostly a story of epic disobedience. God only knows why God keeps at it.

There are, however, a few key examples of faithful obedience in our biblical story. The ultimate paragon is Jesus, who is repeatedly described as "obedient to the point of death" (Phil. 2:8). Though Jesus is plenty capable of getting himself into worldly trouble, he remains fully committed to God against the temptations of Satan, the disloyalty of his friends, the desperate reality of doubt, and even death itself. Trembling in the Garden of Gethsemane, Jesus begs that God might spare him. But immediately afterward, still slick with the sweat of genuine fear and doubt, he prays, "Yet, not my will but yours be done" (Luke 22:42). And dying on the cross, having already cried out in despair (depending on which Gospel account you prefer), Jesus commends his spirit to God and breathes his last (Luke 23:46). In his obedient submission, Jesus enters into death and overcomes it for the sake of us all.

The faithful witness of Jesus Christ cannot be overshadowed or matched by another, but he's not the only major biblical figure noted for his obedience to God. Long before Jesus took on flesh and entered into this world, there was Abraham. After waiting a lifetime for a son, Abraham conceives two. First Ishmael, with his wife's slave, Hagar, and then—according to God's promise—Isaac, with his wife Sarah. Not too many years after the fulfillment of this promise, in a biblical passage known as the Akedah, God says to Abraham, "Take your son, your only son Isaac, whom you love, and go to the land of Moriah, and offer him there as a burnt offering on one of the mountains that I shall show you" (Gen. 22:2).

In response to God's horrific command that Abraham kill his young son as a sacrifice to God, Abraham does not argue. Instead, he gathers his son and packs up the things needed for an altar sacrifice and sets off to follow God's command. Isaac is just old enough to carry the wood for the fire to burn his body. At the appointed time and place, Abraham lays his beloved son on the altar and prepares to sacrifice him. Perfect, unquestioning obedience. And thankfully, God sends a messenger to intervene just in the nick of time. Isaac's life is spared, and Abraham's faith commended. Ever since, we have held up Abraham's obedient willingness to sacrifice his son. Confronted with this brutal story about a God who demands a father kill his own son as a sign of faith, we are challenged to either faithfully accept or disobediently question.

## The Problem of Politeness
### (How Argument Separates Us)

These popular biblical interpretations of Abraham and Jesus establish a Christian precedent for believing that faithful obedience means silent—or at least unquestioning—acquiescence. In this theological framework, passionate refusal or argument is seen as faithless insubordination. However, in the early days of Christianity, the church itself was seen as radical, insubordinate, and conflict-inciting because it refused to submit to Roman religious understandings or place Caesar on the same footing as God.

After Constantine, Christianity became intertwined with the state, and sometime over the centuries a theology of faithful obedience became likewise intertwined with secular notions of proper etiquette. Jesus' Sermon on the Mount proclamation to "turn the other cheek" became conflated with silently bearing one's own mistreatment or oppression. The call to love one's enemies became a call to be nice and polite—no matter how someone else is treating you or others. The call to understand ourselves as a single body of Christ came to be understood as a call to hold together no matter what, and above all, not to rock the boat. Essentially, Christian obedience became a call to adhere to the ethics of civility.

Even in increasingly secular twenty-first-century America, these standards of behavior pervade our culture. Recently, the significance of civility has become a point of particular contention. Though civility originally centered on how to be a good and engaged citizen, sometime around the sixteenth century the word took on a definition more akin to general politeness, which is still its dictionary definition today.[2] The dictionary also notes an archaic definition of "culture; good breeding."[3] This is not an altogether surprising evolution. The word "civil" derives from the Latin *civilis* meaning "of or relating to citizens." Meanwhile, "politeness" derives from the Latin *politus* and evolved from a more literal meaning of "smooth and polished" in a physical sense to one of "elegant and cultured" in the sixteenth century, before finally landing on its current understanding of "courteous behavior."[4]

The not-so-subtle implication of this evolution is that those who were good citizens (i.e., those who were *allowed* to be citizens, especially the elite who had proximity to and influence over state power) established the expected codes of behavior (i.e., behaviors that preserved the status quo), and those with less access to power were left to assimilate to the best of their ability, or else be effectively gated from "polite" or "civil" society.

Over the centuries, this divide along the fault lines of civility and politeness has frequently—if not always—mirrored fault lines of class, race, gender, sexuality, ethnicity, nationality, religion, and so on. Essentially, the crucial function of civility is that it maintain the existing system of power by keeping the privileged powerful and the oppressed "in their place."

This is as true today as it was five hundred years ago.

During the 2016 election cycle, Donald Trump gained the nomination of the Republican Party and ultimately won the presidency largely through the support of working-class white Americans who felt disenfranchised from power and the political system by Washington elites. They and others who supported Trump pointed to his refusal to play by the rules of the system and his willingness to speak in ways that were typically considered inappropriate or rude, as he referred to his opponents as losers and any number of other disparaging descriptors. Essentially, they saw him as helpfully uncivil in a way that reflected their own experience of failing to match the expectations of elite society.

Ironically, Trump defended himself against accusations of incivility by pointing to precisely the ways he differs from many of his most ardent supporters, harking back to a definition of civility that relied on class and status rather than behavior. In a conversation with reporters in October 2017, Trump said, "I think the press makes me more uncivil than I am. You know, people don't understand I went to an Ivy League college. I was a nice student. I did very well. I'm a very intelligent person. You know, the fact is I think—I really believe—I think the press creates a different image of Donald Trump than the real person."[5]

Months later, in the middle of 2018, civility again became fodder for American debate when citizens encountered members of President Trump's administration in public spaces and confronted them with anger and harsh words.

Owners of the Red Hen restaurant in Lexington, Virginia, asked White House press secretary Sarah Huckabee Sanders to leave after Sanders and her friends had been seated and ordered food. The restaurant owner had not been at the restaurant when Sanders first arrived, but her employees reached out to her because they were uncomfortable.

According to the *Washington Post*, the owner said, "I'm not a huge fan of confrontation. I have a business, and I want the business to thrive. This feels like the moment in our democracy when people have to make uncomfortable actions and decisions to uphold their morals."[6]

This situation with Sanders was one of several like it over a period of a few weeks. Trump adviser Stephen Miller was called a "fascist" while dining at a restaurant.[7] Environmental Protection Agency administrator Scott Pruitt was confronted during lunch by a woman with her young son in tow.[8] The woman urged Pruitt to resign, saying, "We deserve to have somebody at the EPA who actually does protect our environment, somebody who believes in climate change and takes it seriously for the benefit of all of us, including our children."

Not long after this encounter, Pruitt did indeed resign, saying that "the unrelenting attacks on me personally [and] my family are unprecedented and have taken a sizable toll on all of us."[9]

These public confrontations sparked a fierce discourse on the definition and significance of civility. While some encouraged the confrontations, many of the most established leaders across the political divide decried the encounters as "unacceptable." Opinion pieces in major newspapers offered various perspectives on who was to blame for the breakdown in public decency. In a *New York Times* piece, Michelle Goldberg argued that people were resorting to uncivil tactics precisely because they were unable to voice their concerns in traditionally civil ways.[10] Though she was speaking in defense of those confronting Trump administration members, it's worth noting that Trump supporters offered similar reasoning for why they voted for him in the first place.

While some claim that civility merely calls us to be respectful in our disagreements—a noble pursuit in general—opinions vary widely on what constitutes respect and who is deserving of it. As long as civility is defined by the existing system of power, arguing or dissenting in any way that destabilizes the system is deemed uncivil.

To the extent that faithful obedience has become conflated with civility and politeness, to be uncivil is to be unchristian. To be unapologetically disruptive is to be unfaithful or ungracious. To be argumentative is to create discord and tension at the expense of peace. Certainly, it's reasonable to claim that the call to Christian life comes with expectations of behavior. We are called to do justice, love kindness, show mercy. We are called to recognize the image of God in other people, even those who we believe are doing ungodly things that harm others. We are indeed called to love our enemies.

However, we must carefully disentangle our Christian understanding of faithfulness from a politics of politeness. It is not our Christian task to preserve the status quo of American ethics, or even earthly ethics. We are called to be anchored, above all, to the ethics of the kindom of God.[11] And when worldly understandings of respectful behavior preserve the power of some by silencing others, we must question whether those worldly understandings match the ethics to which God calls us and which Christ embodies.

Does God call us to hold our tongue, to temper the passion of our argument or the strength of our conviction in the name of civil discourse? To denounce our own anger over that which runs contrary to our deepest beliefs as hateful and thus inappropriate? Does God call us to inflict these expectations on others?

At some point, we must examine our dogged commitment to civility and subsequent fear of argument. What compels these convictions? Is it truly our Christian faith? Or is it merely our human fear of discomfort, conflict, and upheaval?

## Do Talk Back to Me
### (Argument and Obedience in the Bible, Revisited)

Jesus does a remarkably impressive job of engaging nonviolently even with those who seek to do violence to him. Hanging on the cross, Jesus neither uses divine power to save himself nor even curses his executioners. Indeed, he pays them relatively little attention, choosing to focus instead on the two men hanging on either side of him, also facing death (Luke 23:32–43). To these, he offers opportunity for grace and hope.

It's true that Christ follows God's command even to death. But if we look to Christ as our paragon of obedience, we quickly find a framework of behavior that embraces argument and upheaval and, at times, rejects standard expectations of decorum. In the Sermon on the Mount, Jesus instructs his followers to resist anger and seek reconciliation (Matt. 5:21–26). Elsewhere, when those who are paralyzed or suffering physically approach him, he makes time for them (Mark 2:1–12; John 5:1–15). When the hemorrhaging woman interrupts him on the way to visit the dying daughter of an important official, he stops to praise her faith (Mark 5:25–34; Luke 8:43–48). He saves an adulterous woman on the verge of being stoned (John 8:1–11), sits with tax collectors and other sinners (Matt. 9:11), and makes time for meal and fellowship in the face of certain death (John 12:1–10). Remembering these stories, it is clear that Jesus embodies kindness, love, and radical grace which we can only hope to imperfectly emulate.

And yet, he unflinchingly refers to questioning believers and certain corrupt religious leaders as a "brood of vipers" (Matt. 12:34). He decries an entire generation when he is asked to show a sign of his power (Matt. 16:4). He curses a barren fig tree that is unable to sate his hunger with fruit, and when he encounters the money changers in the temple, he flips their tables with no restraint or concern for the rules of civility (Mark 11:12–25). He also makes a habit of rebuking his disciples when they repeatedly miss the point of his teaching. It's clear that Jesus isn't afraid to show anger, to shout when necessary. And though he refrains from physically harming other people and warns his followers against it, he is more than willing to cause a little destruction and disruption when the greedy powers of this world vandalize sacred space.

Jesus does indeed show mercy and grace and seems to recognize the God-belovedness of all those he encounters, including his enemies. But he also sets himself against systems of power and expectations of behavior when they violate his own God-given ethics.

One could suggest that Jesus is allowed to get angry and argue and throw tables because he is the Son of God. Who other than Jesus can know when anger is righteous, and who among Christians would dare to claim that Jesus isn't allowed to argue exactly as he sees fit?

However, in the story of the Syrophoenician woman (or Canaanite, depending on the Gospel account), we see Jesus allow and even praise arguments *against him* in the name of true faith (Matt. 15:21–28; Mark 7:24–29). In both Matthew and Mark, Jesus encounters this woman who is not one of his people, and when she seeks his help he refuses her, saying, "It is not fair to take the children's food and throw it to the dogs." She doesn't quietly desist. Instead the woman pushes further, pointing out that even dogs eat the scraps from the table.

By approaching Jesus at all she has violated social rules. And then she has the gall to argue with him about whether she deserves his help. Rather than scold or rebuke her for her insolence, as he has previously proven himself willing to do with others, Jesus praises the woman for her faith and heals her daughter. Biblical interpreters and theologians debate whether Jesus actually changed his mind or was merely setting an example. But either way, he makes clear that argument can be an act of faith.

Abraham's story too, upon closer inspection, might have a more nuanced theology to offer us than silent, unquestioning obedience—even, and especially, in the Akedah. At the beginning of that story, when God first demands that Abraham sacrifice his son, the text reveals that Abraham is being tested. From a perspective that exalts obedience as the ideal virtue of faithfulness, Abraham's silent acquiescence seems like the correct response to the test. But taken in the larger context of God's interaction with humanity and even with Abraham specifically, it seems that God might have been testing something else.

After all, Abraham has established his commitment to obeying God time and again prior to this test. At God's command,

Abraham gathers his wife and nephew and leaves his homeland for a destination unknown. He refuses to take the spoils of his conquests after battle, he plays the gracious host to God's angels, and he even circumcises himself and all of his men after his covenant with God is made. God has little cause to question Abraham's obedience, given this lengthy résumé. One is left to wonder either why God still needs reassurance or whether this test in the Akedah is about something else. It seems as if, rather than testing Abraham's obedience, God was testing Abraham's faith in their relationship.

Abraham's relationship with God is supremely special, especially in comparison to the other humans with whom God has previously interacted. The covenant that God makes with Abraham not very long before the Akedah story represents a profound shift in God's relationship with humanity. Prior to the covenant, God addresses humans as a master demanding information or action from a slave. God demands answers, asking Adam and Eve, "Where are you?," and Cain, "Where is your brother?" (Gen. 3:9; 4:9). God gives Noah exact specifications for building the ark. Even with Abraham, before their covenant ritual, God simply commands Abraham to go to Canaan, leaving space for nothing other than obedience.

However, through the covenant, God invites Abraham—and his descendants with him—into a new relationship. According to Genesis 17, God promises to establish an everlasting covenant with Abraham and his offspring, out of whom kings will arise, and to whom the land of Canaan is given. In return, Abraham promises to uphold the covenant. As a marker of this relational change, Abram and Sarai are given new names, Abraham and Sarah. When God calls to Abraham in the beginning of the Akedah, it is the first time in the Bible that God addresses a human by name. Through this covenant, God and Abraham enter into a relationship not of master and slave, but of partners engaged in mutual participation and conversation.

The astoundingly intimate and mutual nature of God's relationship with Abraham is even more explicitly revealed in the story of Sodom and Gomorrah, which falls between the covenant ritual and the Akedah. In this story (Gen. 18:17–32), God decides to destroy the sinful cities for their unfaithfulness and reveals the plan to Abraham. He dares to push back on God, bargaining about the number of righteous inhabitants that would allow Sodom and Gomorrah to be spared. God allows Abraham's challenges and, even more strikingly, considers changing plans in response to Abraham's protests.

In the Akedah, God seems almost to be daring Abraham to protest again. Calling for the sacrifice of Isaac is an utterly cruel demand, made even more twisted because it directly contradicts the promise God made to Abraham as a term of their covenant— that his descendants would flourish through Isaac. Elie Wiesel points out, in his essay on the Akedah, that ancient Jewish law would have claimed that God was just as bound by the terms of the covenant as Abraham.[12] Given this, Abraham would have known that God had no right to make such a demand and that Abraham would be absolutely justified in questioning the order.

However, Abraham doesn't question. He doesn't speak at all. Instead, he simply rises early in the morning to set about the task that God has asked of him. This choice marks the beginning of a deep and striking silence that permeates the story and stands in stark contrast to the previously established dialogue. In refusing to speak, Abraham essentially denies his sacred relationship with God.

The journey to Moriah—the place that God indicates for the sacrifice ritual—takes place in unbroken silence for three days. When they arrive, Abraham commands his men to stay behind, and tells them that he and "the boy" will go worship (Gen. 22:5). Abraham's word choice here is significant—he refuses to identify Isaac as his son. Quite possibly, he simply must distance himself in order to carry out the act that lies before him, but in any case, he effectively denies another sacred relationship, that of a father to a son born as the miraculous fulfillment of divine promise.

When Isaac is bound upon the altar, and the knife is raised in Abraham's hand, heaven intercedes to spare Isaac's life. But while it had been the very voice of God who first called out to Abraham in the beginning of this story, it is now an angel who delivers the command that stays Abraham's hand. Abraham chose silent obedience over conversation with God, and here, God refrains from direct conversation with Abraham.

Certainly Abraham's obedience is praised and the angel tells him that, as a result, his descendants will prosper, but underlying these reaffirmations of the covenantal promise is an unspoken and less favorable consequence to Abraham's choice. When the trial is over, the text states that Abraham returns to his men. As Elie Wiesel points out, the singular "he" is significant and intentional in contrast to the "we" stated by Abraham when he and Isaac first leave their servants behind.[13] What exactly has become of Isaac is unclear, but a definite separation has occurred and Abraham is never again described as speaking to either Isaac or God. When Abraham returns home from Moriah, he is a man alone. Where he has denied relationship to God, so relationship is denied to him.

The question lingers: Was Abraham faithful in his silent obedience to God's command, or was more required of him? Was his ultimate duty to the single sacred command or to trust in the relationship?

So eager is Abraham to obey, so afraid is he of defiance, that he upholds God's command even over all his other experiences of God's nature and will. But God is living and dynamic and relational, and to relegate God to one single command is to create a static image of God. In his silent obedience, Abraham has created an idol of his understanding of God's command. We must be wary, in setting our sights on obedience to God's *command*, that we don't lose sight of God's own *self*. We are required to do more. To obey God's will—certainly—but also to encounter and discern that divine will in participative relationship with God.

Perhaps the question is not whether we silently obey or not, or even whether we are quietly polite and thus faithful, or else rebelliously argumentative and thus disobedient. Perhaps the question for us is what to obey and how, and how to do it in ways that foster authentic relationship rather than rigid systems of decorum where people are bound by the strictures of civility or nicety and can therefore only offer some fractured and restrained insight into their convictions.

## Trust Enough
### (How Argument Can Save Us)

In reexamining the witness of Jesus, we see an example of daring and sometimes argumentative engagement both embodied by Christ and encouraged in others when born from a place of faith. In reexamining Abraham and the Akedah, we see a warning against silent obedience at the expense of honest and engaged relationship. The potential cost, then, of avoiding argument when it is needed is loss of relationship, distance, pain, and even death. By contrast, the gift that argument holds for us, if we dare to allow for it in ourselves and in others, is genuine, authentic, honest dialogue, born out of deep trust, from which previously unimagined futures can grow.

Not long after my spiritual encounter with a snake by the creek at my seminary compelled me to embrace my own queerness, I came out to several people I loved. I was still months away from being ready to tell my parents, but I was so alive with this new understanding of myself and the new relationship with a classmate that came alongside that discovery that I had to share.

I revealed my news to two trusted people from my home faith community, a pastor and a dear friend from childhood. To my dismay, neither of them offered the acceptance and embrace that I hoped for. One asked whether I'd considered how much this would devastate my parents. The other pointed to my previous romantic misadventures and questioned whether this new relationship was worth the cost, and went on to say that had I come out as gay they would have been supportive, but that bisexuality felt too much like trying to have one's cake and eat it too.

These trusted friends knew me deeply, and I believe their rejection came both from judgment and from genuine understanding of my history. It was also because of my close and long-term relationships with both of them that their responses devastated me so deeply. I trusted them and their assessment, and I was so new and fragile in my queer identity that I wondered whether they were right. Perhaps I didn't love this new person enough to let my truth hurt my family. Perhaps there *wasn't* any such thing as bisexuality, and I was simply a still-halfway-repressed gay woman.

On the basis of those two painfully sad conversations, I might have walked away from myself and the future of love and authentic queerness that awaited me. Or I might have walked away from these two lifelong friends and the history and love we shared. They might well have decided they were done with me, too.

On the other hand, our years of trusted relationship were also how I found the strength and courage to push back, to trust both myself and them with the scarier possibility that I was right. I responded to each of them, both angry and defensive. My posture was emotional, no doubt, and neither as strategic nor as compassionate as I would have liked. But I left nothing back. In the fury of my pain I bared the truth of that hurt and my own ultimately undeniable convictions to them. It could have been the end of my relationship with either of them, but it wasn't. I stayed in the struggle with them, and they, no doubt out of their love for me and trust in our relationship, stayed in the struggle too. We argued, and we grew, by God's grace, to a place of reconciliation. These days those two old friends are also two of my fiercest allies.

Perhaps those experiences are why, several years later, I dared again to argue with someone I trusted and cared for. I had an uncommonly close friendship with my seminary's president. We connected when I was still a prospective student over our shared history in Atlanta and the South Carolina low country. He sounded like the men I'd grown up around, like home, and beyond that, my mother knew of him and respected him, so I trusted him implicitly. No doubt that is why he was one of the first people beyond my close circle of friends to whom I came out. I no longer remember exactly what either of us said in that conversation, but I know that I expressed fear that the place we both came from and the people in it would never understand and embrace me for who I was. And I know that he expressed, without hesitation, that if indeed it turned out that my people wouldn't have me, he would be my people and he would embrace me exactly as the queer and God-beloved person that I was.

It was a powerful and holy moment. And it contrasted sharply with the tense oppositional circumstances we often found ourselves in over the next several years. My coming out catapulted me into political awareness and activism. I joined a cadre of fellow queer students and our allies in fighting against ongoing inequalities on our campus and in our denomination. My seminary president, for his part, was a self-identified pro-LGBTQ liberal who found himself in the middle of central Texas, which counted a number of conservative Presbyterian churches, both big and small, among its number. Whatever his own ideological mooring, his deepest conviction was in a church that should stay united as one body even amid crucial value differences. The president and I were often at odds over how the seminary should respond to this tense reality. And yet, with a fair amount of frequency I found myself in his office talking about ministry and my future and even, sometimes, the very things that divided us.

Never was this divide between the two us more fraught than in my final semester of school. At the time, our denomination was poised to vote on two deeply controversial issues at its upcoming 221st General Assembly (2014)—divesting from three American companies doing business in Israel, and clarifying our definition of marriage to include same-sex couples. I admit I was so focused on the marriage equality vote that I knew next to nothing about the divestment issue or the politics surrounding it, but it was also a pivotal and controversial vote.

As I mentioned in the previous chapter, in the face of these impending conflicts, Columbia Theological Seminary sent a letter to the commissioners of the General Assembly urging peace and togetherness above all, and they encouraged their sister seminaries to follow suit. Responding to this call, the faculty of my own school also addressed a letter to the commissioners, calling for "mutual forbearance" and the delay of any ruling that might contribute to further conflict and division within the church. Both letters were made public, and they stirred up quite a response.

The outcry against my seminary's letter was swift and potent. Many wrote responses and either sent them directly to the faculty or published them online. I did both, writing about my disappointment that this same group of people who taught me a theology that allowed me to embrace my queer identity and compelled me to seek justice would sign their names to a document that stood against the full inclusion of myself and others like me. I allowed my letter to be published on the blog of a local pastor who was gathering oppositional responses to the seminary's call. Only afterward did I realize that I was the only current student who had published a public response.

My president called me in for a meeting. I was so afraid of the conflict I knew was coming that I had to force my body down the hallway and into his office. I had never seen him so angry, and he was angry *at me*. My southern upbringing and the ways I'd been taught to move through the world as a woman—not to mention my Christian background—told me to calm him down and defuse the situation by any means necessary. But I didn't. I was angry too.

I reminded him of our long relationship and what he knew of me and what I knew of him. And I reminded him that my disappointment in the faculty's letter was valid and that I didn't have a responsibility to silence that disappointment, even if it made him angry. And then I told him honestly that our opposition made me sad because my graduation was the following weekend, and I had been waiting three years for my mom who so respected him to meet him and see someone who knew all that I was and was proud of me not in spite of my queerness, but in light of it. There were tears, I think.

And though nothing was resolved and we were both still angry, he promised me that the following weekend he would do what I had hoped for. And he did. I listened as he sang praises about my preaching to my mother and I watched her light up and tell him confidentially that I might be one of the best preachers she'd ever heard (moms are allowed to say that sort of thing).

One month later, in the minutes after our General Assembly voted to approve an inclusive definition of marriage by overwhelming majority, I ran into my seminary president in the hallway of the convention center. Our recent and freshly relevant argument hung between us. But so did everything else. We hugged. And he said, swallowing hard, "This is a good day. I am scared as hell. But this is a good day."

Our conflict and argument were one part of a much larger conflict in our church that is still not fully resolved, and I sometimes doubt it ever will be. But I am grateful for both the conflict and the honesty it allowed to grow between me and this mentor I cared for.

There is no obvious perfect answer for how we go about faithfully threading the needle between gracious engagement and genuine, trusting argument. I know that the answer is ugly and hard and preserves no one's comfort. But I love to imagine a world in which we might trust in God and ourselves and this world enough to lay it all on the table. To unflinchingly bear our arguments and our passions and our vehement disagreements and bear the fiery truth of others'. Not to value our perspectives or even deepest moral convictions more highly than others' humanity, but perhaps to value the possibility of honest engagement and mutual relationship they offer more highly than we value others' comfort, or our own.

There is immense risk in embracing true argument, in not allowing our fear of conflict or our desperate reliance on systems of civility to silence others or ourselves. We can only discover the extent of that risk in actually doing this scary thing. In shouting it out, in bearing it all. But there is risk in silence too. Silence costs us and that cost is, I believe, all the more fearsome because the thing about silence is that what it costs, we never get to know.

We are called to more. I believe we are called to ongoing sacred dialogue. And to be in sacred dialogue is to question, to challenge, to struggle—with God and one another, and even, at times, with ourselves. We are called, in blessed contradiction to what all the grown-ups taught us, to talk back.

*Chapter Four*

# The Gift of Tension

There is a teaching in Judaism called "The Two Pockets" that is generally attributed to Rabbi Simcha Bunim, who lived in Poland in the first half of the nineteenth century. The teaching goes something like this: Everyone should have two pockets. And in each pocket, one should have a slip of paper. On one paper, in one pocket, should be written, "I am but dust and ashes." On the slip in the other pocket should be written, "For my sake, the universe was created."

My best friend Robin taught me that story from her own Jewish upbringing. The point, as I understand it, is to bear in mind, constantly, our significance and our insignificance. To live in the space between the two. Essentially, to persist perpetually in the tension between two opposing but somehow simultaneous realities.

Of course, I've had my own experience of learning to live with tension, learning how to exist in the midst of multiple opposing but simultaneous realities. I joke that I am bisexual because I don't like binaries or borders or overzealous boundaries. But the truth is, I believe that being bisexual—even in the years before I knew that's what I was—has taught me to be comfortable with tension and to not jump too quickly to an either-or resolution. Being bisexual means loving in a way that many people say is impossible. We are told that you either love one gender or another. Bisexuality says it's not that simple: I can love multiple genders. Because I am a bisexual woman who tends toward dating men, I've also had to learn how to exist in the tension between my very real experiences of struggle, judgment, and discrimination—and the advantages I have over many other LGBTQ people because my life fits more easily into a heteronormative-appearing framework. And of course, being bi also means living in the tension of being a part of the LGBTQ world without ever being entirely accepted in it. Bisexual people face judgment and rejection by both straight people and gay people. Some say we don't exist, others say we have to choose, others say we just don't want to admit we're gay or that we're straight but want to pretend we're not.

These tensions aren't fun, but they are part of what it means to live in this world as a bisexual person. And I have found that it has made me a person who knows how to hold two seemingly opposite truths in one hand at the same time. It also allows me to accept such paradoxes in others. It's taught me to question "if . . . then" logic, to resist assuming that if one thing is true then another can't be, or that if one thing is good or right then another must be bad or wrong.

Of course, it isn't just bisexual people who have to deal with tension. We all live in the cross fire between seemingly opposed realities all the time. So much so, in fact, that we are rarely fully aware of them. We love our children and cherish time with them, and also crave a break. We love our families and find them exasperating. If we're lucky, we love our work even when it is endlessly frustrating or we dream of doing something different one day. We can be passionate about something and it can exhaust us or cause us anxiety. When we find ourselves in the crosshairs of such paradoxical truth, we accept that a part of life and love and existence is being in tension. And not just temporary tension either. It's true that sometimes we deal for a time with multiple irreconcilable realities because we can see the light at the end of the tunnel. We know the tensions will one day be resolved. But there are other tensions with which we simply learn how to live. We are but dust and ashes, and yet, somehow, for our sake the universe was created.

## Our Binary Obsession and Why It's a Lie
### (How Tension Separates Us)

Despite the fact that we acquiesce to unresolved tensions known and unknown on a daily basis, we don't like tension, as a rule. We may accept it as a necessary evil, but it feels uncomfortable and unstable. In fact, if we're trying to name how tension separates us, the reality is that tension is literally the space between two opposing things. It is the elephant in the room at family dinners, and awkward first dates, and the first time you hang out with a friend again after a big fight. Our instinct is that tension is an obstruction to be overcome and fixed, preferably as quickly as possible.

Generally, when tension can't be easily resolved, we avoid it. We keep our distance from the spaces and relationships and situations that have too much tension. We make our home in what feels easy and clear and not up for debate. As a species—or perhaps merely as a culture—we are immensely fond of clear delineations, of black and white, of either-ors. We are inclined toward binary thinking. I suppose this is because it's simple and reliable. If only one of two things can be true, then we can assume that if one thing is true, the other is not. If one thing is right, then its opposite must be wrong. If one thing is good, then its opposite must be bad. Binaries give us a sense of certainty. Tension gives us the opposite.

The problem with this is that a whole lot of the things we assume are binary are not. We assume that a person's sex is either male or female, but science tells us that's not always the case. People can also be intersex. Those of us who rely on a binary understanding of sex find this truth uncomfortable. We fear that if this binary isn't real or isn't so simple, other certainties we've assumed based on it—like, for example, the relationship between sex and gender—might also be more complicated. So we pretend it doesn't exist. We claim that it's a lie, or an anomaly so insignificant that it's not worth acknowledging. We say, "Even if there are a few exceptions, the world can still be divided this way." But guess what? It can't. Not really. It's more complicated than that—there's a tension there.

There are countless other examples of our habit of assigning binaries where they simply do not belong. I learned to read at age three and first declared that I wanted to be a writer at age four. All through school, English and language arts were my favorite classes. Somewhere along the way, somebody taught me that everyone is either an English and history person, or a math and science person. I guess this is based on some kind of aptitude tests, but it has seeped into our understanding of who a person is.

Since I knew that I was an English person, I concluded that I couldn't also be a math and science person. Going into high school, I applied for a special science program for high school freshmen at the Fernbank Science Center in town. The program allowed students to spend half their school day at the center, doing intensive hands-on science learning. The application required a very brief paragraph about why I was a good fit for the program. I was fascinated by everything about the program, but the first line of my answer was, "I'm not really a science person, so I think it could be good for me to be challenged in this way." Unsurprisingly, I did not get accepted, which of course only further confirmed my belief that I was not a science person. My need for math tutors later in high school confirmed that I couldn't be a math person either. I continued my path as a clearly defined binary person and majored in English in college.

Years later, I took on a position that was part-time teacher and part-time data analyst for a nonprofit that provided extended school day programming for middle schoolers. The data part of the job required a fair amount of math and statistical analysis. I took on the responsibility because I wanted to challenge myself in an area that I knew wasn't a natural fit for me. Except as it turned out—it was. I loved the math and the number-crunching and the data analysis as much as I loved the more qualitative and language-based parts of my job. And I was good at it! For the first time it occurred to me that maybe I didn't have to be either an English person or a math person. I could be both.

I suppose believing that I was one or the other had allowed me to focus my attention and development in certain areas, and there's value to that. But what had I missed by spending years believing that I couldn't be a certain thing because I was another thing instead? False binaries give us false certainty and false limits. They restrict what we're capable of believing and understanding and even being.

We tell people that they must be either introverted or extroverted, male or female, intelligent or unintelligent, successful or unsuccessful. When we say someone is spontaneous we also mean that they are not a planner. When we say someone is a big-city person, we assume that also means they are not a rural person. We actually love dividing ourselves and others up in these ways. Since the 1990s the internet has been chock-full of quizzes that tell you who you are based on whether you like lakes or the ocean or the mountains or the desert, whether you like to travel or stay at home, whether you like big crowds or intimate gatherings.

Then, having thoroughly defined ourselves and others by what we are and what we are not, we divide ourselves into groups and communities based on what we share in common. Those who don't share those commonalities are "different" and "other." The more that we define ourselves and our world in this way, the less capable and comfortable we become with the idea that maybe it's all more complicated than that. Maybe we are more complicated than that.

Tension isn't exactly the opposite of binaries—that would be a false binary in itself. But a world that can't be so easily split into either-or is also a world that isn't so easy to understand or resolve. And that blurry, unresolved, nonbinary space—that is tension. Doing the work of reckoning with false binaries means recognizing that tension is everywhere, even inside us. And if that's the case, then we have to learn how to live with it.

## Wrestling Angels and Holy Unholy Bets
### (Tension in the Bible)

The Bible doesn't exactly have books or chapters that explain how we—as people of faith—should deal with the tension that exists in our lives and our world. But it does say a thing or two about staying in hard, unresolved places and learning to exist in the absence of easy answers. In fact, the reward for this kind of behavior seems to be divine blessing.

The book of Job is a hard story. In my opinion, it doesn't make a particularly strong case for God's benevolence or for the benefits of unflinching faithfulness. Job is a righteous man with bountiful blessings. God shows him off to Satan, and Satan replies that Job is only faithful because of all the good things God has given him and that if those things were taken away, he would curse God. God argues that Job would remain faithful and righteous no matter what. Thus a bet is made, with poor unsuspecting Job caught in the crosshairs.

With God's permission, Satan takes from Job his wealth, his servants, his children, and finally his health. In the face of each new loss, Job says, "The Lord gave, and the Lord has taken away; blessed be the name of the Lord" (Job 1:21). With their lives overcome by pain and grief, Job's wife tells him to "curse God, and die" (2:9), but Job continues to defend God.

Job's friends sit with him in his grief and misery, but they are convinced that he's being punished by God for something, and so they tell him to repent. But Job knows that he has done nothing to deserve what has befallen him, and so he insults their lackluster loyalty. Except that finally, Job is angry enough to cry out to God. He doesn't renounce his faith or curse God's name, but he does ask why all of these terrible things have happened. God sort of dodges the question, but offers an epic poem about the vastness of creation and the expansiveness of God's knowledge and power. Job relents, acknowledging that he cannot fully understand the mind of God and that there is much more going on than his own sorrows.

Essentially, Job arrives at a place of understanding that the universe was created for his sake and that he is but dust and ashes. Job's faithfulness isn't about black-and-white thinking. In fact, he is able to remain faithful precisely because he resists the impulse to impose binaries and false correlations. He is able to believe, somehow, that God is good and that God can allow terrible things to happen to him. That he can be righteous and still suffer. Job knows that he can be both faithful and angry, that God can hold both. In fact, what Job seems to understand inherently is made even clearer in God's whirlwind speech: the universe is vast, God is complex, and the answers are rarely simple. Multiple truths can and do exist all the time, and the space of tension between these opposing and challenging truths is where true faith resides.

Jacob also seems to understand tension and multiple truths. He knows that faith sometimes means not just recognizing tension, but wrestling with it, and holding on to it, and staying in it. In Genesis, Jacob is both wily trickster and heroic Jewish forefather. The Bible tells us that even in the womb he was fighting his twin brother, Esau. Later he tricks his brother into trading his birth-right for some stew, and then he tricks his father, Isaac, who is blind, into believing he is his slightly older and much hairier twin so that Isaac will give Jacob the blessing that is reserved for the older son. Later, his wiliness shows its face again in his dealings with his uncle Laban, who has a few tricks of his own up his sleeve.

By all accounts, the biblical narrative doesn't paint Jacob as standard virtuous hero material. And yet, he becomes father of twelve sons from whom twelve tribes descend, and so Jacob becomes the entire nation of Israel. The truth is that there's a reason Jacob is the way he is. He is born into a rough world as the second—and less favored—son of his father. His people lead hard, nomadic lives, surrounded by pharaohs and famines and slavery and war. Jacob learns quickly that the world isn't simple or full of easy answers. He learns that two seemingly opposed things can be true at once. He can be the second, less favored son of his father, and the person whom God has chosen to become the father of God's own people. He can be a faithful and honorable man, and a wily, dishonest trickster. In fact, to follow the path God has laid out for him, he must be. Jacob lives in the tension of these irreconcilable truths.

Of course his tricks have a cost. He gets a taste of his own medicine from his uncle Laban. He is separated from his beloved mother and fiercely at odds with his brother. And this last one is why he finds himself, eventually, staring down an inevitable and terrifying reunion with his brother Esau. He is once again mired in tension, feeling both fear of and love for his brother.

The night before he and Esau are set to encounter one another, Jacob gathers up his family and his people and sends them across the Jabbok along with everything he has, and then, the text tells us, he is alone. Except all of a sudden, he isn't. A man is there— the text doesn't tell us how the man arrives or who he is—and he and Jacob wrestle until daybreak.

As the story in Genesis 32 goes, when the man realizes that Jacob isn't going to give up and that he won't prevail against him, he strikes Jacob's hip socket and puts it out of joint. Then the man tells Jacob to let him go because day is breaking, but Jacob refuses. "I will not let you go, unless you bless me," he says. And so the man asks Jacob's name and blesses him, telling him, "You shall no longer be called Jacob, but Israel, for you have striven with God and with humans, and have prevailed" (Gen. 32:28).

When Jacob asks the man's name in return, he simply says, "Why is it that you ask my name?" And then, apparently, the man is gone, and Jacob names the place Peniel, saying, "For I have seen God face-to-face, and yet my life is preserved." And as the story ends, Jacob leaves that place to face his brother Esau, limping because of the injury to his hip—a permanent reminder of his encounter.

I wonder, reading the story, how Jacob knows that the man he encounters is God. Perhaps it's because the man appeared out of nowhere or because he offers Jacob a blessing. Or maybe it's because really, what other random stranger would show up in the middle of the night to wrestle with you until sunrise?

Regardless, this encounter is intimate and intense. It's incarnational, relational, and mutually vulnerable. These two men, or one man and one supreme being, are grappling with each other's bodies. In fact, the word translated here as "wrestle" literally means "to get dusty."[1] They are rolling around in the dirt together, getting dusty. This word choice takes on even more meaning when you remember God's declaration to Adam and Eve that they were created from dust and will ultimately be returned to dust. Whether you take that verse as a condemnation or as a promise of ultimate restoration and reconciliation, God and Jacob are rolling around and wrestling in the midst of the messy tension of humanity, both created for good and fallen.

All through this long night, while Jacob waits in the unresolved and uncomfortable space of his impending reunion with Esau, God stays with Jacob. Pushes Jacob, and lets Jacob push back. God is in the struggle with Jacob. Though Jacob has had to spend his entire life on guard, holding people at a distance with his tricks and deceptions in order to survive and pursue God's call on his life, in this moment of dusty intimacy God reminds Jacob of the power of relationship. This encounter is not one easily categorized. It is a fight, and it is a dance. It is about opposition and intimacy. It is about fighting for yourself and embracing relationship. It is about prevailing, but it is also about the struggle.

When God sees that Jacob isn't going to give up, Jacob finally earns the blessing for which he has asked. God says to him, "You shall no longer be called Jacob, but Israel." And the reason? "For you have striven with God and with humans." Striven. Wrestled. Gotten dusty with. God is honoring Jacob not simply because Jacob won, but because he was willing to struggle at all, to dare to engage and involve himself, to be fully in relationship, to be impacted. In fact, "Israel" literally means "to struggle with God." What makes Jacob strong is that he doesn't settle for easy resolution. He wrestles. He gets dusty. He *stays* in the struggle. In the messiness of relationship. In the tension. For as long as it takes.

The struggle has its impact on Jacob, of course. The text tells us that as he leaves that place of holy encounter, he is limping because of the injury to his hip. His encounter, his striving, literally changes the way he moves through the world, perhaps forever. Resisting the temptation to give up or settle for easy answers or disengage—all of it—changes a person. It leaves a mark. But it also offers a blessing of growth, of promise, of bigger possibilities.

## What Holy Looks Like, When Resolution Cannot Be Found
### (How Tension Can Save Us)

Naturally, the gift that tension has to offer us isn't an easy one to receive or accept. Tension doesn't give us anything easy or gentle or simple at all. Quite the opposite. When we resolve to acknowledge the tension that is everywhere—all around us and within us—what we get is complexity. With complexity comes struggling to understand, comes a lack of clarity, comes discomfort. But complexity also brings with it nuance and depth and an expansive world of possibilities for us to exist into, that we can't see with a strictly binary, either-or lens. Tension, when we stay with it long enough, shows us there is always more to the story.

Twice in the last several years, I have made trips to Northern Ireland to learn about the country's conflict-ridden history and complicated intertwining between religion and politics, most recently for a story that was published in *Sojourners* magazine.[2] To say that circumstances in Northern Ireland are complex and tension-filled is a massive understatement. A friend once compared it to an analysis he'd heard of the conflict in Israel and Palestine. If you go for a week, you'll think you don't understand it at all. Stay for a month, and you'll think you have it all figured out. Stay for a year, and you'll know you will never fully understand. That resonates with my experience in Northern Ireland. It is an incredibly beautiful and hospitable country, and it exists, seemingly forever, in the midst of powerful and deeply rooted tension.

For most of Northern Ireland's history, including before it was its own country, it has been defined and weighed down by an intense and complicated conflict between Catholics and Protestants. Though the conflict has been drawn along religious and sectarian fault lines, and uses religious language, it is not so much about religion as it is about politics and civil inequalities. Centuries ago, England recognized that Ireland's proximity made it a risk, and so the British government made strategic efforts to colonize Ireland, sending Protestant settlers from England and Scotland (who would become known as Scots Irish) to establish themselves in the most fertile and accessible parts of Ireland, all the while pushing the native Irish Catholics out. In fact, the Irish were prohibited from owning land under British rule.

When the Republic of Ireland was formed in 1920, Britain retained the northernmost part of Ireland—a region known as Ulster that had been seen as a particularly strong threat—and made it the British-ruled country of Northern Ireland. The Catholic Irish in Northern Ireland overwhelmingly opposed

British rule and considered themselves Irish Nationalists, while the Protestant descendants of British colonizers were Unionists who supported the crown. The centuries-long hostility between the two groups continued as the divisions between them became formalized in the function of government. The Irish Nationalists were deemed dissenters and thus the loyal Unionists were given advantages and preferential treatment in terms of voting, housing, employment, and other civil realities.

As tensions mounted in the 1960s, paramilitary groups developed and clashed against each other and the police. Ultimately, Northern Ireland saw three solid decades of profound violence and unrest—shootings, bombings, and murders claimed countless lives of Catholics and Protestants alike. These acts of violence were met with protests and food strikes and imprisonments that added more names to the long list of lives lost in this period that, these days, is referred to by the rather understated term "the Troubles."

Based on my own experience, if you ask a Northern Irish person about the Troubles, they'll be reluctant to say very much. On the one hand, there's a tendency to downplay it—on the other, a rather heavy reckoning. Nearly everyone I've met from Northern Ireland knows an entire list of people who were lost. While working on my story for *Sojourners*, I spoke with a woman who had been a member of a Catholic church in Belfast for thirty years. I asked her what resolution and justice looked like. She told me that, in a world where nearly everyone has seen someone they love murdered—what *can* justice even look like at that point? What can peace and reconciliation look like in a world where true justice and resolution aren't possible?

Of course, I have no answer—I cannot imagine what life is like for people in Northern Ireland, especially those who lived and lost through the Troubles. As my friend observed, I have been there just long enough to know that I will never fully understand. But there is a place in Northern Ireland, a community called Corrymeela, that commits itself to the work of exactly what the woman I met in Belfast named: how to exist and coexist in the midst of tension that might never fully find resolution.

Corrymeela was started in the 1960s by Irish Presbyterians, though these days it claims an identity of "all faiths and none" and boasts members and volunteers from all over the world. It sits on the rocky cliffs overlooking the Irish Sea on the northern coast of Northern Ireland. It isn't a giant place, a collection of five or six buildings, including a dining hall, housing, a greenhouse, and a round, odd-looking little chapel called the croí, which means heart in Gaelic, where non-religion-specific services happen every morning.

Corrymeela has, since its inception, sought to respond to the tension and conflict that permeates life in Northern Ireland. Its founder, Ray Davey, had been a prisoner of war in Dresden when it was bombed during World War II, and the experience impacted him profoundly. He began to think about what it would mean to build community in the midst of conflict. Later Davey served as Presbyterian dean of residence at Queen's University, and when sectarian conflict began to escalate in the 1960s, Davey and some of his students decided to form a community in Ballycastle, Northern Ireland, where "all people of good will" could come together. Corrymeela continued its work of community amid conflict throughout the Troubles, and they have found, over time, that it requires a nuanced and long-term approach.

One of Corrymeela's hallmark programs is an annual weekend for widowed parents. For many years now, these parents have been invited to bring their children to the beautiful campus of Corrymeela for a weekend away from the stresses of their daily lives. The staff and volunteers provide programming for the children so they can have some fun with other kids who know what it's like to lose a parent. Meanwhile, the widowed parents are given time to meet, share their stories and struggles, and support each other. The families invited include Catholics and Protestants and those on all sides of the sectarian divide. The staff I met with during my visit to Corrymeela explained that, at the beginning, they don't talk at all about the Troubles or the ongoing tensions and divisions that exist in Northern Ireland. They talk about the experiences they share, the struggles that they can intimately empathize with one another about. Over time, relationships develop. And eventually, the previously unnamed tension point comes up. It's generally not a profound revelation or dramatic conversion but someone simply observing, "I know Protestants are this way, I've known it my whole life—but you're not like that." Or vice versa.

It isn't a cure-all. History is still history, and though much good has happened in the two decades since the Good Friday Accords put a formal end to the Troubles, there are still systemic biases at play. It isn't a solution or a resolution. In some ways, it's the opposite. What happens for these families at Corrymeela is recognizing the humanity in one another, which centuries of conflict had made it nearly impossible to see. In these relationships and glimpses of one another, these folks find a way to exist in the face of an ongoing—or at the very least, lingering—tension that, in their lifetime, may not ever end.

Corrymeela is a "thin place." When you're there, you feel all around you that the Holy Spirit is present, that what happens there has the mark of God on it. It isn't a perfect place—nothing so clear-cut as that—but precisely because it holds space for the unresolved, it is holy ground.

## In Conclusion, Don't Rush to Conclude

I'll admit, I have a bias here. I have lived in the midst of tension my whole life. I've already talked about how this has played out for me as a bisexual woman. Meanwhile, being southern means that the region I call home and love with all my heart is also one with a terrible history and very real problems in the present. As I discuss in the next chapter, on separation, growing up in a blended family meant living in the tension of multiple people's pain and broken relationships, even while finding my own joy in the same reality. Being Christian and queer requires remaining in the tension of my deep conviction that God loves me as I am and my knowledge that many in the church believe that who I am condemns me to hell—and some have done great violence to people like me in the name of that belief. Being a liberal from a conservative upbringing sometimes means navigating the tension between my firmly entrenched values and my relationships with the people I love most.

Our impulse toward tension says that these various tense realities must be resolved. I must choose: Christian or queer? One side of my family or the other? Love the South or acknowledge its painful truths? Maintain the integrity of my convictions or compromise on them to love my family? I believe that the truth is more complex than that.

To be clear, embracing tension doesn't mean having no nonnegotiables. Acknowledging complexity and resisting the urge to resolve tension doesn't mean, "Yeah, I believe murdering someone in cold blood is wrong, but I guess maybe it's also right." And it also doesn't mean compromise. People have grown fond, at least in my circles, of saying we have to "live in the tension." But too often, people use it when they really want to say, "You should be willing to compromise." Compromise on your conviction in the name of relationship. Compromise on justice in the name of peace. Compromise on truth in the name of politeness. I'm not saying that there's never a time for compromise—of course there is. But make no mistake, compromise isn't staying in the tension. It's resolving it.

Compromise says, "Resolving this tension is more important than anything else—more important than what either of us really wants." Staying in the tension does mean not demanding an either-or, but it also is saying, "Maybe we shouldn't compromise or fight to the death. Maybe we should stay here in this complexity for a while." While the phrase "agreeing to disagree" seems to hint at a willingness to stay in tension, too often it means "let's not talk about the very real tension between us anymore because it's uncomfortable." Like compromise, this phrase can often be used to force a resolution where one doesn't belong. The truth is that when it comes to other people, staying in tension requires relationship. Staying in relationship doesn't mean being in agreement or even being peaceful or nice to each other. It doesn't mean relinquishing our convictions. It means staying engaged, whether you're in the same room or not. It may not mean constantly fighting, but it does mean not ignoring what puts you at odds. And, of course, just as sometimes compromise can be a right answer, sometimes staying in relationship can be a wrong one. Sometimes we can't be in relationship with others and be in good relationship with ourselves. Sometimes we *do* need an either-or boundary.

The point here is not to claim tension as a universal good or a universal ideal, but we should know that it isn't a universal bad either. It isn't something that is always in need of remediation. If we only accept a world of either-ors, then we miss the chance to encounter the God of both-and. A God who wrestles and embraces, who speaks in a whirlwind and in a gentle silence, who is large enough to create the vastness of the universe and intimate enough to create and love each of us. A God who is somehow both one and three, and somehow both human and divine. Accepting these unresolvable tensions is a crucial cornerstone of our theology. When we run from tension, push it away, or rush to resolve it, when we settle for black-and-white easy answers, we also miss the chance to encounter the God-given complexity in ourselves, and in others, and in this world.

It is part of faith to strive, to struggle, to wrestle and get dusty. To live somewhere in the midst of being dust and ash, and ones for whom the universe was created. It is both our gift and our responsibility as complex creatures to stay a while in unresolved places and question whether there is a deeper and more complicated truth—or multiple truths—to be discovered and held and honored. We live in a world of tension, and we were made for it. We need not be afraid.

# The Gift of Separation

If you're going to write a book arguing that there are gifts to be found in the very things we fear because they separate us, then sooner or later you have to consider the concept of separation itself. Is there any good to be found in separation? Many would argue that separation—even when necessary—is always lamentable. We grieve breaks in relationship and departures, whether temporary or permanent. We wonder how we've become so divided and what we can possibly do to bring everyone back together. Of course, there has never been a time when we were *all* together. And I'm not at all convinced there ever will be—at least not in this world. And I'm not sure that's entirely a tragedy. Yes, separation often means pain and heartache. But even separation has gifts to offer.

My mom and dad divorced when I was two years old, and my mom married my stepdad when I was four. I have no real memories of life before these two things happened, which is to say, I have no real understanding of life that isn't colored by separation. I suppose there's a sadness in that, but it mostly didn't feel that way to me. I grew up with two homes, two families, and—in many ways—two different lives. To me, that mostly felt like spaciousness, like room to expand and explore life in different ways.

Of course, I was confronted with the difficulties of divorce and the particular challenges of growing up in a blended family.

I learned early how to navigate tense relationships and felt responsibility for managing situations that weren't mine to manage. But I also experienced how good things can grow from separation—I got new sisters and cousins and a whole extended family that I wasn't born with. And I developed a uniquely close relationship with my dad because so much of the time, it was just us and my brother.

It must be acknowledged that what felt like a gift to me was painful to others. And of course, it helped that I never knew anything different. My point is not to claim that separation isn't painful or is never bad. Divorces, breakups, farewells, schisms—separation nearly always carries a profound degree of pain. But we often speak of separation as if it is the outcome we must avoid at all costs, an overwhelming tragedy, a failure. My experience says that isn't the whole truth. Spaces of separation can also be fertile soil where new and previously impossible things can grow.

### Separation and the Bible
### (It's More Complicated Than You Think)

According to the Bible, our human story begins with a series of profound separations. First, when God creates, that which is created is, in some ways, separate from God. Then God separates various parts of creation from one another—separating the sky from the sea, land from water, dark from light. And then God sets man apart by giving him the role of caretaker. In the Genesis story, God then separates one of Adam's ribs from his body in order to make woman. In explaining the role of this partnership, God decrees that henceforth when two people choose to share life together, they must become separate from their families in order to become bound to one another. And, perhaps most profoundly, God gives humanity free will, separating forever our choices from God's will. We can align with God's will, but we are not bound by it. We are separate.

None of these early separations are presented as negative, though free will shortly has its own massive repercussions. As discussed in chapter 1 on the gifts of difference, these first separations are what allow creation and relationship to exist at all. In separation, Adam and Eve and the various parts of creation are allowed to fulfill their specific roles. In theory, everything could have continued on, separate but connected, in peace and gentleness forever. In theory.

Instead, these divinely intended separations are soon followed by further separations that are not God's will and cause great pain and cleaving. At the serpent's urging, Eve eats of the forbidden fruit and then Adam does the same. When their eyes are opened, they choose to turn away from their relationship with God, and they hide. Then when God calls them out of hiding, Adam separates himself from Eve by blaming her, and Eve separates herself from creation by blaming the serpent. As a result, Adam and Eve are made to leave the garden, to toil for their sustenance, to experience great pain in childbirth, and to be enemies of the serpent.

Even after this massive parting of ways, the biblical story tells us of other separations. Cain rises up against his brother Abel. Noah and his family are separated out while the rest of humanity is destroyed. After years of following Abraham around, Lot goes his own way to settle elsewhere. Hagar is cast out into the desert with her son Ishmael, away from Abraham, Sarah, and Ishmael's half brother Isaac. After the near sacrifice of Isaac, Abraham and his son are never shown to speak again. After stealing a birthright from his twin brother, Jacob leaves home and spends twenty years away with his uncle Laban, and then runs from Laban as well. Joseph's jealous brothers sell him into slavery in Egypt, and they do not reunite for many years. Moses is sent down the river by his mother to spare his life. While Ruth clings to her mother-in-law, Orpah chooses to return to her own people. The examples go on and on.

Indeed, the Israelites' entire story is one of separations— separated into different tribes, separated from their homeland during the Babylonian captivity, separated from God by their continued failings in regard to the covenant. Many of their laws existed to maintain separateness—no intermarriage, no mixing of different foods or materials. And then Jesus comes into the story.

And maybe one would think that the Son of God, the Prince of Peace, would bring about an end to separation. And in some ways he does. He challenges societal notions of acceptability that separate out people like tax collectors and sex workers and lepers and make them pariahs. He rejects deeply entrenched divisions between Jewish people and others, like the Samaritans and the Syrophoenicians. In his final moments, he offers a command and a blessing to his mother and his disciple, that they become one family (John 19:26–27).

But Jesus doesn't bring about the end of separation. In fact, he charges his followers to set themselves apart from the world. In the Gospels of both Matthew and Mark, he comes upon fishermen—first Simon (called Peter) and his brother Andrew, and then James and John, the sons of thunder (best descriptor ever, by the way). And in both tellings of the story, the text says that Jesus walks up to these guys who are making their living and commands them to drop their nets and follow him (Matt. 4:18–22; Mark 1:16–20). And they do! Right then and there, they abandon their nets, their livelihood, and their communities, and they follow Jesus. Awkwardly, in Luke's Gospel Jesus goes so far as to say, "Whoever comes to me and does not hate father and mother, wife and children, brothers and sisters, yes, and even life itself, cannot be my disciple" (Luke 14:26). And then we know that Jesus himself was unwelcome in his own hometown, and says that the same is true of any prophet (Luke 4:24).

Separation is not only present in Christ's ministry and in his call to faithfulness, it's crucial. To be of faith is to be set apart. When Jesus has died and been resurrected, the time comes for him to ascend to heaven, and though he has entered into humanity itself and even broken down the doors of death, Jesus separates himself from us once again. "Where I am going, you cannot follow me now," he tells us, but then he goes on to say, "You will follow afterward" (John 14:36). Our theology doesn't free us from the reality of separation—not now anyway—but it does promise that all that has been separated or torn asunder will one day, in the world to come, be restored.

## Separation and the Church
### (It's Even More Complicated)

It's fair to say that, if the Bible's perspective on separation is complicated, the church's is a whole lot more so. Early in the fourth century, Emperor Constantine issued the Edict of Milan, which made Christianity, for the first time, not a criminalized religion. For most of history since that auspicious occurrence, Christianity has been powerfully aligned—either explicitly or implicitly—with the state in much of the Western world. In this Christian-centric paradigm, Christian faith has been both expectation and obligation. Identifying as anything other than Christian sets one apart in a way that often means at least judgment, if not outright marginalization. Even today in America, with numbers steadily declining in most Christian denominations and a general sense that religion is dying, Christian influence on culture and government still runs deep. This version of Christianity—the one that holds court as the status quo—is fearful of any kind of separation from state or cultural influence that might detract from its power. This Christianity is used to a world in which to be Christian is to belong. ´

Of course, it hasn't always been that way. The early church more closely followed Jesus' instructions to be set apart from the world. It helped that early Christians were largely persecuted for refusing to worship Caesar or the Roman pantheon. And early Christian ascetics like the desert fathers took separation to a whole other level, removing themselves from society and its luxuries entirely. Modern monks still live out this impulse to pursue faithfulness by separating themselves from mainstream society.

But even within Christianity, separateness has existed nearly since day one. Peter and Paul were the church's earliest leaders, and they spread the gospel to different populations in different places, with somewhat different foci. Peter kept his attention on Jewish people and observances of Jewish law. Paul, by contrast, made a point of reaching out to Gentiles. Their differences often put Peter and Paul at odds with one another, but one could argue that their different convictions and commitments were key to Christianity's early growth.

Even once the Christian church was well established—and government sanctioned, for that matter—divisions stirred it up from the inside. The first few centuries of Christianity's existence saw intense debates over who was and was not a heretic and what was and wasn't the nature of God and Christ. The most contentious debates were addressed to be settled via a series of seven early ecumenical councils that took place over a period of five hundred years.

Perhaps the most lasting result of these councils was the Nicene Creed, which was meant to be an ecumenical theological declaration agreed upon across Christianity. And yet, for all their meetings, profound disagreements persisted across Christendom, ultimately leading to schisms between and within the Eastern and Western churches.

Then, of course, there was the Protestant Reformation. Though he had predecessors, Martin Luther and his Ninety-five Theses are largely credited with launching the Reformation in 1517. Luther's intent was to reform rather than break away from the Catholic Church, but his ideas ultimately led to a profound and lasting separation between Protestant Christianity and Catholicism. He was joined by Huldrych Zwingli and John Calvin, and from their various movements, and reactions against them, countless separate Christian denominations and traditions have been formed.

In many traditions, including my own Presbyterian/Reformed tradition, splits of varying size and intensity have been occurring ever since. A massive split occurred between the northern and southern Presbyterian churches in the United States over the institution of slavery. The denominations would later reunify, but not until 1983—more than a century after the Civil War, and not before yet another branch of Presbyterians, called the Presbyterian Church in America, had broken off over the ordination of women. Other mainline Protestant denominations have seen similar splits and schisms over the years, with only the occasional reunification.

Most recently, in my own denomination, there was significant controversy over the questions of whether LGBTQ people could be ordained and whether their marriages would be recognized and allowed by the church. After decades of often extremely contentious debate, the Presbyterian Church (U.S.A.) voted to allow the ordination of LGBTQ people in 2011, and later to include same-sex couples within their definition of marriage. In the midst of these changes in denominational policy, a number of pastors and congregations dissented. Some, attempting to stay in relationship in the midst of disagreement, formed the Fellowship of Presbyterians. Others broke away completely, and a new, small group was formed, the Evangelical Covenant Order of Presbyterians, which still approves of women's leadership—just not anyone LGBTQ.

In the final years of these debates, as departures from the denomination were increasing, a lot of denominational leaders and others within the church campaigned for folks to stay together at all costs. They spoke of the tragedy of no longer being willing to sit in the same pew or stay at the same table because of theological differences. These days, much of the same conversation is happening in the United Methodist Church, which seems to be drawing nearer and nearer to a split over LGBTQ inclusion.

Though I don't believe formal separations should be entered into lightly, there's no point in denying that separation is in our DNA. There have been splits, departures, and divisions in the church since the beginning. And however much someone might say they grieve that fact, whenever someone sits comfortably at home in the pew of their own denomination, they are in some way benefiting from whichever series of separations allowed the Christianity they identify with to exist. It's time to consider that maybe none of us really believe that separation is entirely a bad thing. It's time to consider that separation has its own blessings to bear.

## Blessings to Bear
### (The Truth of Separation and How It Can Save Us)

It's interesting to me that we talk about separation in the church as if it's an epic tragedy, and not just because so much of the modern church exists because of separations that have happened in the past. It's also because we actually *don't* consistently view separation as a bad thing in our culture. There are separations we're encouraged to try to avoid, such as divorce, even if they do turn out to be for the best. But other separations are literally seen as a rite of passage.

The most obvious example of this is probably leaving home. We send our kids off to college or out to live on their own. Granted, parents talk about the hardships and sorrow that accompany such a shift, but those hard feelings are generally coupled with pride and joy and excitement. We recognize that it's important for children to separate from their parents, and we start these separations in small ways: handing them off to a babysitter, sending them to kindergarten, letting them go to a sleepover. Eventually, kids leave entirely. The Dixie Chicks have an entire song about the significance of such a separation. "She needed wide open spaces," they sing, "room to make a big mistake."

Learning how to be independent is part of becoming an adult, and independence requires certain degrees of separation. When someone fails to separate effectively in this way, we call it codependency, or we simply label it as "failure to launch" and make a rom-com about it starring Sarah Jessica Parker and Matthew McConaughey. On a more serious note, countless articles have been written about the millennial generation's arrested development and extended adolescence, largely marked by an ongoing dependence on their parents.

So if we generally view separation as a bad thing, why have we made it such a key milestone of life? What makes us value the kind of separation that comes from setting out on your own and establishing independence? In short, I think the Dixie Chicks have it right. We need space. Though it's worth noting that not all cultures valorize the notion of the individual as an ideal state or priority, in mainstream American culture, self-differentiation is at least as important as commitment to community. On some level, we recognize that it is hard to become your own person—to learn how to take responsibility for your own thoughts, actions, and well-being—without some kind of separation or independence. Whether that means a move across the country or just out of the house, we understand that some kind of space is required for growth.

Growing up in Atlanta, I was lucky to be exposed to a lot of experiences different from my own. While I grew up in a conservative Christian Republican family that was comfortably upper middle class, I attended school and activities, sports teams and summer camps, with people of other faiths, other political alignments, other income levels and family structures and worldviews. I had the privilege of traveling internationally at a young age and seeing cultures and ways of living far different from my own. These experiences stretched and challenged me, and they broadened my imagination, all in ways that might not otherwise have happened for someone who mostly aligned with the privileged norm—which is to say, saw my own narrative reflected in mainstream movies, TV shows, and literature.

Still, on some level, I knew that I was different in some important ways from the people I loved most and the primary community that surrounded me, even if I didn't understand entirely what those differences were or how I felt about them. I needed to get away and travel my own path for a while. The diversity of lives I was exposed to in my youth made me aware of how big the world was and how expansive the possibilities of humanity were, but until I had gotten out into that world, I wasn't able to sort out exactly where I fit in it all. For me, this meant that after college I moved a thousand miles away to Texas to do several years of full-time volunteer service. Having the means to do so was, itself, a privilege. And not everyone's version of setting out on their own looks like that. I'll also admit that I don't know if there is the same pressure to strike out and find space to grow for those who largely align with their family or whose cultures place more emphasis on family and community loyalty than individualism. But however it looks, most of us embrace separateness in one way or another. It's just a part of life. And that is not necessarily a bad thing.

When I came out—to myself and a few close friends, at least—early on in my first year of seminary, it immediately raised questions for me about my connection to my home church in Atlanta.

I was still a member at the church my family had joined when I was six years old, the church that had been the singular constant for me over all the years of shifting between two homes and families, various moves, friend groups, awkward phases, and so on. Even if I knew I needed to go on a journey and figure out who I was apart from the world I'd grown up in, I still felt more at home and known and comfortable with myself in that church community than anywhere else—except when it came to my sexuality, which felt as if it had the power to destroy the very comfort and belonging I'd come to rely on in that church.

I had been attending and actively participating in a church in Austin for a while already when I decided to attend seminary and pursue ministry. In fact, one of the pastors of that Austin church had met with me regularly through my discernment process. It was this newer church that had shepherded me back into faith after several years of angry disconnection, and I had made another kind of home there. Still, my love for my childhood church ran deep, and the knowledge that they were so hugely responsible for my faith development and my call to ministry made it seem only right that I should be under their care during my official ordination process. When I met with their session—that is, the governing committee of church members—to get their approval and support in pursuing ordination, I was looking mostly into smiling faces I had known almost my entire life.

Several months later, when I finally acknowledged to myself that I couldn't pursue a call to ministry without being fully honest about who I was, I started to wonder if those same people would still be smiling once they knew. Honestly, I feared the worst, but I really wasn't sure. I knew that my church was ideologically diverse and that we had largely managed to coexist by avoiding conversations that were too controversial. And I knew the senior pastor who had come after I moved away was much more conservative than his predecessor, but also always seemed kind and was well liked.

In many ways, I wanted to push this community I loved to consider their stance on LGBTQ inclusion, and I thought their long-standing love for me might allow space for such a loaded conversation to happen. But I was newly out and very scared, and I wasn't ready to sacrifice these relationships and this home I'd known on the altar of my convictions, even if I should have been. More importantly, I was far from ready to come out to my parents, and it felt unfair to throw a truth bomb like the one I was holding into a community a thousand miles away and leave my parents and other people I loved to deal with the aftermath of the explosion while I went about my life in Austin.

I made the decision to leave the care of my home church and transfer both my membership and my ordination process to the church I'd been a part of in Austin, which self-identified as progressive and affirming and had a tendency to welcome in queer seminarians who came from more conservative places. I didn't tell the full truth about my reason for leaving—not then. I talked about the difficulties of distance and my desire to walk through the process with a congregation I could regularly be involved with. That was reason enough on its own, and my home church let me go with their blessing.

Over the next several years, I returned often to my childhood church for holidays and school breaks. They always welcomed me, eager to hear updates about my ministry journey. I never had an open conversation about my sexual identity with anyone there beyond my parents and my former youth pastor. But I was fairly public online and I trusted that, by the almighty power of the church grapevine, many of them knew. The senior pastor never mentioned it and was always warm and encouraging to me, even though we hadn't overlapped during my time in Georgia. And over time I began to wonder if I'd made a mistake in leaving, if they would have been up for the challenge and stood behind me. If nothing else, I took some comfort in the fact that it had never become an issue.

In the months leading up to my graduation from seminary, after I'd secured a pastoral residency in Chicago and my future ordination seemed almost certain, I decided that maybe it was time to go home. It was customary in my childhood congregation for children of the church who had gone on to enter ministry themselves to come back and preach. So I reached out to the pastors and asked if I might do so while I was home that summer. For a while, I heard nothing back. And then the answer came. I had a long conversation on the phone with the senior pastor. We went back and forth. He told me it was too heated a time (just weeks before I was due to be home, our denomination would be voting on whether to include same-sex couples in its definition of marriage and allow pastors to officiate at their weddings). He told me it was for my own good. He told me that he was sorry, but it just wouldn't be appropriate to allow me into their pulpit. He was very polite.

I was crushed. It was the first time that I knew for sure that my sexuality was a barrier in my relationship with my home church. It was the first time I knew that even though this church had so firmly instilled in me a belief that God loved and accepted me as I was, they could not, at least not officially, and not everyone. It was the first time I knew for sure that I had made the right choice in leaving. What had previously felt like a blurry line took clear shape as an unscalable wall. It was an incredibly hard reckoning.

Just a few months later, my denomination did indeed vote to pass marriage equality, and shortly thereafter the senior pastor of my childhood church sent a letter to his congregation, stating his own inability to stay either in that church or in the denomination, given this new theological position. And he left. He moved to Florida and became a pastor at a church that was part of the Evangelical Covenant Order. His departure was hard on a lot of people. Some were sad to lose him and sadder still because they had counted on him to help them make sense of the changes in the denomination. Others were angry that he would give up and sacrifice relationships rather than stay. And still others were mad because they disagreed with his reasoning. Some left when he did, for reasons similar to his. As for how I felt about it . . . Honestly? I was relieved. Not because I wish him any ill will—I didn't and I don't. But because as long as we were struggling to belong in the same denomination, I wouldn't be able to be fully part of my church home. Neither of us would ever be able to engage in church without it feeling like a battle.

My mom grieved his departure. She was really struggling with the church's ongoing and ever-deeper engagement with what, to her, seemed like political issues. She was hoping that her pastor would help her understand why she should stay.

I remember the day in 2014 that our denomination voted in favor of marriage equality. I was there, sitting in the spectator section of our denomination's biennial General Assembly. In my section, I was surrounded by other LGBTQ people and our allies. Some of them had been in the work of advocating for inclusion in our denomination for decades. They had lost friends and loved ones who had also been in the work and died long before their hopes ever became a reality. When the first vote—allowing ministers to officiate at same-sex weddings in states where they were already legal—came through in our favor, there was a restrained sort of quiet joy. No one was allowed, in that space, to have vocal positive or negative reactions. A little while later, the second proposal—an amendment to the denomination's constitution that clarified the definition of marriage to include same-sex couples—passed by a stunning majority. The gasps were so many and so widespread that they dominated the space. Around me friends wept and laughed and hugged. One friend, a middle-aged gay man, looked at me with tears streaming down his face and a giant smile, and he said, "I have to go call my husband."

I clutched my chest as pain tore through it, and I sobbed too. Almost all of my reaction was from unexpected joy. But some of it was for my childhood church and the knowledge I already had that this vote meant their pastor would leave. And some of it was for my mother, who I knew might leave too.

I waited three days to call her. The night of the vote, I gathered in a fancy hotel suite with friends and we toasted the occasion and told stories of all that had happened to lead us to this day, and named the names of those who hadn't lived to see it happen. The following weekend, when I was back home, I dialed her number. We exchanged casual pleasantries. I told her about my experience that week, skirting the obvious. And then I asked her how she was feeling about the votes that had happened, not only the LGBTQ votes but also others related to Israel/Palestine and abortion access. My remarkably stoic mother paused and I could swear I heard her breath hitch a little, and then she said, "I just feel like my church is leaving me behind."

I remember how close I came to saying what I was thinking, "I know, but we don't want to." My mother didn't leave. Not then. She didn't go to services much, but she taught Sunday school as she had for over a decade. A few years later, she and my step-dad moved full-time from their home in Atlanta to Hilton Head Island, South Carolina. They began attending a traditional and conservative Episcopal congregation there, and a few months ago they became members. Am I thrilled that we are so ideologically different that we can't be at peace in the same church? No. But I am happy to be in a denomination that affirms my identity. And I'm happy that my mom has a place to go to church too.

I have always been puzzled by more moderate friends who seem to think that, because they hold the middle and call for unity, they alone truly care about friends and loved ones at either end of the spectrum. Whenever I hear arguments like this, I think, "Are you kidding me? Do you know who is at the other end of this spectrum? It's my mother, and I'll be damned if I allow you to suggest that you care more about her than I do."

It isn't that I don't wish, deeply, that my mother and I could be equally at peace in the same church. It's that I know that it takes at least as much love and commitment to look in the face of one of the people you care most about in this world, and to know that at this time you cannot be theologically reconciled, and to let them go to pursue faith in a way that doesn't prevent you from doing the same, hoping all the while that your paths might one day come together again. For all the ways we disagree, my mother and I have both done that for each other.

So much of the talk about holding together seems to come from a place of fear. The fear, best I can tell, is that if we no longer claim the same denomination, our relationship will be permanently severed. It's as if, somehow, the second someone walks out of our church, our responsibility to them ends. And frankly, that's just not what we believe. Whether we claim the same logo, denomination, church, or not, we are bound up together in love of the same God and in that God's love for us. If anything, I worry that our fear of letting one another go comes from doubt about the larger truth that God holds us together regardless.

I'll admit, I'm equally as cynical about those who come from families and communities with whom they've never been at odds who propose that faithfulness means being ready and willing to cast a person we vehemently disagree with out of our lives forever. I have known friends who had to make such a choice for their health and well-being. I don't envy them, and it's clear to me that a choice to separate in that way brings a fair amount of pain. But I have found that, in my own life, sometimes walking separate paths has been the only thing that has allowed me to stay in relationship in the midst of profound difference. It is an uneasy, tense, and utterly unresolved space. But dare I say, it is still a beautiful place—worthy, to me, of holding onto.

Sometimes, we choose to walk separate paths for a time so that we can grow fully into the people God is calling us to be. Sometimes those paths lead us back together. I was ordained in November 2014, roughly six months after I asked to preach at my home church and was denied. Just shy of a year after my ordination, I returned home to my childhood church to preach at the culmination of their stewardship season. I preached about the role that a church could and should play being home for people, the role that church played for me, and I also talked about the importance of knowing that church and faith can evolve in ways we cannot imagine and that our call as Christians is to be open to it. I called that sermon "Homecoming," and it was. I was received graciously and with open arms. My mom sat front and center.

Still, at other times it's important to acknowledge that separation may have no clear end point or easy resolution. I don't know if my mom and I will ever attend the same church again, let alone theologically align. Certainly, I have my doubts that the theological differences that separate the various Presbyterian denominations from one another, and different traditions from one another, will be resolved in my lifetime.

But here's the thing: What we claim to have faith in is not a God who settles for imperfect and disingenuous earthly unity. We believe in a God who promises that—no matter what ways this life separates us from one another—we will ultimately be reconciled. I don't see this theological truth as a challenge. I see it as a comfort. And a reminder that we need not be afraid. That regardless of whether faith calls us to walk separate roads for a time or for a lifetime, we are still bound for the same home, and the same homecoming.

*Chapter Six*

# The Gift of Vulnerability

In June of 2010, a previously little-known research professor of social work named Brené Brown stood on a stage in Houston, Texas, and delivered a TEDx talk called "The Power of Vulnerability."[1] In her talk, Brown made the bold claim that the key to whole-hearted living, as she calls it, is a radical willingness to embrace vulnerability. That in order to be loved, we have to risk letting ourselves be seen.

Brown's claim clearly resonated with folks. The video of her talk went viral, and it's now been viewed more than thirty million times. Brené Brown has become a household name, and she's published a whole slew of best-selling books that attempt to explain to people how to lead with vulnerability in their lives. She's even developed a popular training program that helps individuals and groups work to let go of shame and live courageously and vulnerably.

On the one hand, Brown's incredible rise to fame and the viral success of her work speak to a modern claiming and celebration of vulnerability as a virtue. Given this, perhaps it doesn't seem so surprising to suggest that vulnerability is a holy gift. On the other hand, the novelty of her message points to just how deeply entrenched we have historically been in a cultural understanding that vulnerability is weakness and detached impenetrability is strength. Brown's cult following suggests both that vulnerability has transformative power and that we are desperately hungry for it.

In the same year that Brown's first TEDx talk went viral, an artist named Marina Abramović performed a 736.5-hour piece at the Museum of Modern Art called *The Artist Is Present*. From March 14 to May 31, every day, all day long, she sat silently on a chair at a simple wooden table, with an empty chair across from her. Visitors were invited, one at a time, to take their place in the other chair, and Abramović would look them directly in the eyes, unspeaking and focused entirely on them, for as long as they wanted to sit there. She didn't move or talk or judge.

Over the course of the exhibit, Abramović sat with 1,545 people. Most people stayed with her for less than five minutes, but others remained for long periods of time. Some came back more than once. The exhibit attracted celebrities, including Alan Rickman, James Franco, Bjork, and Lady Gaga. A number of times, visitors broke down in tears while at the table, overcome by the experience of being so fully seen. Often, Abramović wept with them. By the end of the exhibit, people were lining up overnight to make sure they had a chance to sit with her. And when it ended, Abramović quietly rose to her feet while a huge crowd of people cheered.

It says something both alarming and profound when merely gazing at someone with your full attention is so rare and atypical that it's considered performance art. And it says something both alarming and profound that people are so compelled by the notion of being fully seen, and fully seeing someone else, that they would wait all night in line for the chance to do so, even for only a minute.

In 2015, after learning about Abramović's performance piece, I preached a sermon on vulnerability, which I ended by asking the congregants to spend thirty seconds looking into each other's eyes. To this day, my former colleague who led worship with me that day gives me a hard time about that experimental move and how uncomfortable it was. In theory we understand that there is value—even necessity—in allowing ourselves to be seen, in making ourselves vulnerable, and in bearing witness to vulnerability in others. But we are simultaneously overcome by the risk of it. We are, in this way, like a person dying of thirst with a cup of water in hand, more afraid of quenching our thirst than we are of death.

## Vulnerability Avoidance, Toxic Power Paradigms, and Oppression
### (How Vulnerability Separates Us)

It's no wonder, really, that vulnerability terrifies us. It is, by definition, a dangerous proposition. Whether we mean physical, emotional, or spiritual vulnerability, to be vulnerable means to be at risk for harm, pain, failure, loss, catastrophe, and any number of other devastating possibilities. Etymologically, it is inherently negative, defined as susceptible to danger, wounding, and attack. And when the kind of vulnerability we're talking about is letting other people—people who have real potential to hurt us— see those convictions about which we are most passionate, those truths about which we are most sensitive, the damage is irreversible. When truth is known and seen, it can never be unseen. And while judgments and evaluations may change over time, the wound they can cause at first blow leaves a stubborn scar.

Vulnerability separates us from one another precisely because we cannot avoid vulnerability unless we also avoid each other. Vulnerability avoidance requires us to limit what we share with others. There are topics we can't discuss, levels of emotion we cannot display. There are fears we cannot name. Beliefs we cannot fully express.

In our desperate attempts to avoid vulnerability, we convince ourselves and teach our children that power looks like subjugation and dominance, that protection of oneself means making others fear you, that violent strength is better than weakness. At its worst, this can look like toxic forms of masculinity, like supremacy, like violence.

Here's the thing: if the way to avoid vulnerability is to be aggressive, dominant, and conquering—one has to have someone else to dominate, conquer, and subjugate. The key, then, has not been to eradicate vulnerability entirely (which I argue is impossible because it is a part of being human, earthly, mortal), but rather to make sure that those around you are more vulnerable than you are. Historically, humans have inflicted vulnerability on others through slavery, imprisonment, subhuman legal status, violent conquest, annihilation, even daily discrimination. We still do. And this reality of forcing the vulnerability of some to preserve the invulnerability of others has contributed hugely to the ongoing and deeply destructive conflicts and divisions in our world.

Whether it's segregation, exclusion, or inequality on the basis of race, gender, sexuality, class, or any number of other identifiers, when the sense of security of one person or group of people is dependent upon denying, diminishing, or desecrating the full humanity of another person or group of people, we are avoiding vulnerability by imposing it on others. This type of subjugation and oppression makes those who do not share the dominant identity vulnerable in multiple ways. It limits access to resources like food, health care, jobs, education, voting power, financial security, and community support, and all these inflict vulnerability in ways both tangible and intangible. It also encourages a cultural perception that some people, by virtue of either innate or culturally constructed identifiers, are to be feared or considered less than others. And these deeply entrenched prejudices also make people vulnerable to violence and hate.

Any conversation about vulnerability as a gift absolutely must recognize the way that vulnerability has been violently inflicted on people by others. This is not a gift. It is a crime. And when vulnerability is forced and weaponized, it only serves to further separate us from one another. The powerful and positive opportunities that can come from embracing vulnerability can only flourish when vulnerability is truly mutual, entered into by the free choice of both parties.

## Virtual Vulnerability in the Virtual Age

Despite our fear of vulnerability, the hunger people feel to be willingly vulnerable persists, as demonstrated by the success of both Brené Brown and Marina Abramović. In the ubiquitous rise of social media over the last couple of decades, human beings have found a way to simulate or manipulate the experiences of willing vulnerability, while maintaining the safety of relative distance.

The internet and social media have collapsed an entire globe of distance into a handful of incredibly popular platforms and an infinite-seeming number of websites, all accessible with barely the move of a finger. We have constructed a virtual universe, complete with virtual relationships and virtual vulnerability. This modern reality is not without its benefits. Thanks to the internet, a young queer teenager living in a small, isolated, conservative community can connect with other LGBTQ people and allies, without fear of physical harm or harm to their relationships. The web allows people to hear about and understand the experiences of people half a world away, with whom they would never otherwise come into contact. And it gives people who share common experiences a chance to connect and exchange stories. Genuine lifelong friendships have developed in this virtual universe. Communities have been constructed. Revolutions organized.

In October of 2016, shortly after news came out about a recording of then presidential candidate Donald Trump bragging about grabbing women "by the pussy," writer Kelly Oxford tweeted an invitation for women to share their first experiences of assault, and shared her own.[2] Within twenty-four hours, Oxford said that she had received more than eight million replies. Her single tweet became the nexus of an overwhelming onslaught of stories of sexual violence, assault, and harassment. Stories ranged from the painfully standard to the nauseatingly horrific. Ages at first assault ranged from barely past babyhood to adolescence. Some women revealed that they'd never shared their story before. The sheer volume of confessions was profound and newsworthy.

I was one of them, briefly.[3] As the momentum built around Oxford's tweet that weekend night, I typed out a 140-character version of my own childhood assault story. I hit Tweet and waited for several long moments, staring at my screen, before I deleted it. In the end, I shared a single number: the age I was at the time of my assault. I remember the feeling of putting even just that much information out into the universe. It felt equal parts wrong and terrifying and somehow also courageous and relieving. It was a short, simple tweet, sent out into the anonymous ether. But just as others' vulnerable stories had power for me, I believe mine had power too. And collectively, our vulnerable sharing became part of a larger movement that has had real, tangible impact.

However, when it comes to truly experiencing and embracing vulnerability, the internet provides as many challenges and road-blocks as it does advantages. While I deeply believe that genu-ine, authentic connection can occur online, it takes a great deal of intentionality and openness to encourage and maintain the level of real vulnerability it requires for transformative relationship to develop. For most of us, most of the time, what the internet pro-vides in the way of vulnerability is . . . a cheat. We are given space to pour out our thoughts and feelings, theoretically to be received by others. But we don't have to sit in that uncomfortable tension of watching someone receive and be affected by our vulnerability. And when we encounter others being vulnerable online, we can know it on an intellectual level, but still avoid the experience of sitting with someone and watching them open themselves entirely before us. Our virtual vulnerability online is mitigated by the tan-gible barriers of our computer screens.

In my work as audience engagement editor for *Sojourners*, I saw the shadow side of what internet connection allows. In the comments section of our website and Facebook pages, and in our email inbox, our readers—many of whom feel ideologically iso-lated in their physical communities—find a sense of connection and encouragement that they are not alone. However, I also saw people be truly heinous to each other behind the safety of their computer screens, often in the same breath that they made some claim of superior faith or morality. Sometimes, I responded to emails that were particularly angry or mean just to let the person on the other end know that their words were received by another human being. In many cases, the emailer wrote back immediately and apologized for their tone, saying something along the lines of "I just got carried away—sometimes it feels like I'm screaming into a void and no one is listening."

Even when every attempt to be vulnerable or receive someone else's vulnerability online is thoughtful and intentional, there is a gap that impedes the value of vulnerability as something shared and mutually transformative. I do believe there are moments online when these barriers and gaps are successfully navigated and overcome, but more often than not, the internet provides a space where we can temporarily sate our desire to be vulnerable without opening ourselves fully or actually experiencing vulnerability in any lasting, transformative way. It can be a start, but it is not enough.

### Flaming Shrubs and Broken Alabaster
### (Vulnerability and Solidarity in the Bible)

While there is plenty of evidence that we hunger for vulnerability, the world around us doesn't explain why. Evolutionarily speaking, avoiding vulnerability seems like a natural pathway to survival. Our faith, however, offers an alternative perspective—indeed, an alternative command.

Long before we encounter the one whose power, we're told, is "made perfect in weakness," we encounter a Hebrew God who, for all the lightning bolts and mighty plagues and victories won and sacrifices demanded, nevertheless seems dedicated to drawing near to us. The God of the Hebrew Testament is one who shows up on mountaintops and in the guise of strangers, wrestling angels, and flaming shrubbery.

And God doesn't just seek out ways to draw near to us. God also asks that we draw near in return. That we open ourselves to God and become vulnerable. Take Moses, for example—he of the pyrotechnic plant. God reveals Godself to Moses in a burning bush. God calls out to Moses, compelling him to come closer. And then, suddenly, God instructs him, "Come no closer! Remove the sandals from your feet, for the place on which you are standing is holy ground" (Exod. 3:5). Perhaps Moses' shoes were dirty. Or perhaps, as many have suggested, removing one's shoes on holy ground was a tradition. But maybe, also, God wanted to be closer to Moses. Without his sandals on, Moses can feel every tiny pebble that he steps on as he moves nearer to the bush. He can feel the sand and dirt between his toes. And we might imagine that he can also feel the growing heat from the flames of God.

Without his sandals, Moses is . . . vulnerable. He can't make a quick escape. He can't tell himself that none of this is real. He can't pretend not to be involved. His body is in it—feet first, and so is the rest of him. Moses is vulnerable, but God doesn't leave him alone in that vulnerability for long.

Moments later, Moses rather daringly asks God's name. This was no minor polite exchange. In Moses' context, as in many ancient cultures, knowing someone's true name meant having power over them—it meant that they were vulnerable to you. Even a god. And yet, God says to Moses, *ehyeh asher ehyeh*—revealing God's name to be "I AM WHO I AM" (3:14). And so together, in mutual vulnerability, God and Moses meet on that holy ground. Perhaps that shared vulnerability is what makes the ground holy. Only in this shared space can God fully convince Moses to lead the Israelites to liberation. Only in that delicate space can Moses recognize God as one to be trusted. And only in allowing himself to be vulnerable can Moses fully discover the strength to do what his faith is asking of him.

This God, who has met Abraham and Isaac and Jacob and Moses and David, comes to us all as a Messiah who defies every expectation of power and salvation. The grace and love embodied by Christ are not defined by power over another, dominance, aggression, or subjugation. Instead Jesus makes his mark on this world through solidarity with those he encounters—especially those who are particularly vulnerable: widows, children, and those cast out by society due to disabilities, illnesses, or origin.

In Jesus, we see a God desperate to be reconciled with us who chooses to do so not by force, but through relationship. A God who so desires to be near us that God would take on the confines of human flesh—and not just any human flesh, but that of a tiny infant born to an unwed mother. A God who so understands the human struggles of this life and this world that, even though he holds the power of resurrection within himself, he weeps at the death of his friend Lazarus, and trembles in the garden, and cries out on the cross. A God who can stand to be corrected when he errs in denying healing to a Syrophoenician woman's daughter, and dares to learn and grow and praise the mother's faith.

Jesus isn't subtle in the way he defies traditional understandings of power and might. In the Sermon on the Mount, he instructs his followers to turn the other cheek, to love and help even one's enemies. To overturn the destructive powers of this world through radical mercy, love, and openness. In the ever-growing shadow of the cross, he dares to ride into Jerusalem on a donkey in a procession of palms. Scholars tell us that this entrance likely occurred across town on the same day as a Roman military parade complete with armor and horses and spears. The message is clear: this is no standard earthly circumstance, and no standard earthly messiah. Everything we thought we knew about the strength that can transform and save the world is wrong.

It isn't just that Jesus Christ embodies power through solidarity and vulnerability. He also asks his disciples to embody those things. In Mark 8:34, for example, Jesus tells those gathered around him, "If any want to become my followers, let them deny themselves and take up their cross and follow me." In typical flawed human fashion, we have for many centuries allowed this verse—among others—to suggest that faithfulness means silently embracing one's suffering. But the cross of Jesus Christ isn't ultimately about *his* suffering, though he does suffer. Jesus' living and dying and resurrecting—all of it—is about Jesus choosing to be with us in *our* suffering and pain. Even when he could choose to escape or avoid it. More than that, by sharing in our struggles, Jesus can overcome our brokenness in ways we just can't on our own, and never could.

The call to "take up your cross and follow me" isn't about silently embracing or even enduring our own pain. It's about allowing ourselves to be open and vulnerable to the struggles and humanity of others. Rather than turning away and protecting ourselves, we are called to stay and be with them, just as Jesus enters into vulnerable humanity to be with us. This idea of letting ourselves be vulnerable, letting ourselves feel the pain of others and have ours felt, is a frankly terrifying thought in this oh-so-very-broken world. And that is why it requires faith in the one we follow.

In this same passage, when Peter rebukes Jesus for speaking about the suffering and death he will undergo, Jesus snaps back at Peter, "Get thee behind me, Satan! For you are setting your mind not on divine things but on human things" (8:33). Jesus is warning Peter that earthly conceptions of power do not align with the way of Christ. The path of faith is one of vulnerability and solidarity.

In Mark 14, when the woman at Bethany breaks open the alabaster jar of perfume and anoints Jesus' feet, she, too, is embracing vulnerability and solidarity. While the other disciples rebuke her for wasting wealth that could be spent in service to the poor, Jesus tells them to leave her alone. He says, "For you always have the poor with you, and you can show kindness to them whenever you wish; but you will not always have me."

These other followers have heard Jesus' command to love and serve those who are poor. But they see it as an issue to be dealt with, a line item in the budget. The woman with the jar—who, by virtue of her association with a leper and her own gender status, is already at the outskirts of society—knows that Jesus' call to care for others in their vulnerabilities isn't about checking them off a to-do list. It's about being fully and truly present with them. In this moment, the woman bears witness to and chooses to share in Jesus' vulnerability. He and she know that he is staring in the face of death. Her act of anointing him is a precious and intimate act of care.

The woman knows that there's a cost to this kind of mutual vulnerability. For her, it is the loss of both the expensive perfume and the approval of those around her. So when she breaks open that jar, she is allowing herself to be broken open too. She gives herself entirely to Christ—honoring him as messiah, teacher, and one who is soon to die. She sees him in all that he is and chooses radical solidarity and vulnerability with him in a way that many of the disciples will soon fail to do. Just as Marina Abramović sat fully present with each of those more than fifteen hundred people, so the woman with the jar sits fully present with Christ.

Holy things happen in spaces of shared vulnerability. The very space itself becomes holy ground. And we find that whether we are speaking to a burning bush, or taking up a cross, or breaking open an alabaster jar, when we allow ourselves to bear witness to others' vulnerability and humanity, and allow them to bear witness to ours, we are in the company of God.

## Risky Business
### (How Vulnerability Can Save Us)

In *The West Wing* episode "Noël"—my favorite episode ever—Deputy Chief of Staff Josh Lyman is suffering from post-traumatic stress disorder (PTSD) several months after being seriously wounded in a shooting. His friend, boss, and mentor, Chief of Staff Leo McGarry, finally forces Josh to see a therapist. Josh is resistant. When the therapist diagnoses Josh with PTSD, he replies nervously, "That doesn't sound like something they let you have when you work for the president."

When Josh finally has a breakthrough and the therapist releases him, it's late at night. And yet he finds Leo—who has been through his own deep struggles in the past—waiting for him in the hallway. When Josh questions this, Leo tells him a modern parable about a guy who has fallen in a hole. As the story goes, a series of people walk by, and the man calls out to them for help. First a doctor passes, and his only help is to write a prescription and throw it down in the hole. Then a priest walks by, and when the man calls out to him, "Father, help me!" the priest merely writes down a prayer and throws it to him.

Leo goes on: "Then a friend walks by, 'Hey, Joe, it's me, can you help me out?' And the friend jumps in the hole. Our guy says, 'Are you stupid? Now we're both down here.' The friend says, 'Yeah, but I've been down here before and I know the way out.'"

Josh Lyman knows that in our modern world, power and security leave little space for weakness. But Leo McGarry knows an

even deeper truth—real power and security come from vulnerability, solidarity, trust, and relationship.

The gift of vulnerability is the ability to be our authentic selves
and to see others' authentic selves. In this space of authenticity,
trust grows and deepens. When we hold back, when we closely
guard and protect the parts of ourselves that matter most—our
deepest convictions, fears, hopes—we deny ourselves the opportunity to be seen and understood and loved for who we truly are.
And because maintaining those walls for ourselves perpetuates
a world that relies on those walls, we deny that opportunity to
others as well. When we embrace mutual vulnerability, we are
mutually impacted and transformed by one another's humanity.

I mentioned earlier that oppression and prejudice inflict vulnerability on people. It's important as we come to recognize the
gifts within vulnerability that we also recognize that forced vulnerability is not a gift. It isn't mutual. And it isn't holy. It's violent.
We exist in a world today where many people are vulnerable—
physically, mentally, emotionally, relationally—not as a matter of
choice, but as a matter of circumstance and exploitation.

Those of us who have largely been able to choose whether we
are vulnerable, who have mostly benefited from the protections
of institutions, systems, and communities, come to the notion of
choosing vulnerability from a relatively safe and untraumatized
perspective. But so often, as we seek to create spaces for shared
vulnerability, we expect those who have had vulnerability inflicted
upon them in one way or another to make themselves even more
vulnerable for the sake of mutuality. We can't do that. Or at least,
we won't achieve the kind of mutuality that makes vulnerability
holy by ignoring the ways others have encountered vulnerability
as a weapon.

Faith calls us as the church, as Christians, as those trying to
embody the love and grace of Christ, to cultivate communities
where people always encounter vulnerability as an invitation and
gift met with genuine mutuality, and never as an exploitative or
imbalanced expectation. As long as we live in a world that inflicts
and exploits the vulnerability of some, we cannot expect vulnerability from those folks for the sake of mutual growth. We all

have work to do, eradicating exploitative systems and deeply entrenched dynamics of prejudice. Part of recognizing and receiving the gift of vulnerability is to deconstruct systems and perceptions of power that avoid vulnerability for some by imposing vulnerability on others.

In the meantime, affinity groups and communities of those who share similar struggles are their own gifts—their own refuge from the storms and devastation of exploitative power. They allow space for people to be vulnerable by choice, alongside and with those who, in the same way as them, have been forced into vulnerability by power differentials and systems of privilege. In these spaces, people of color, LGBTQ people, women, people with disabilities, and others can be honest and vulnerable *about* their experiences and their feelings, without needing to worry about those with more power and privilege who find their feelings threatening because they challenge the status quo. These spaces also allow for a break from the pressure to constantly educate others about one's own experiences.

Sometimes, even at our most well-meaning, those of us who occupy spaces of comfort or dominance within the systems around us, but who are trying to learn and grow and be better, are inclined to believe that the only way to move forward is for us to listen to those who experience struggles and oppression we don't and learn what it's like to be them. The truth is that we can never fully understand, but even as we try to learn and grow, it's just as important that the folks we're learning from have their own spaces to let their guard down, share safely, and experience authenticity and trust for their own benefit. Sometimes, strengthened and supported in such dedicated spaces, those who've experienced vulnerability only as a forced reality are better able to share their experiences with others.

Six years ago, during the summer between my first and second years of seminary, I found myself in the mountains of North Georgia attending, for the first time, a retreat for emerging Presbyterian LGBTQ church leaders, which we affectionately called "secret gay church camp." At the time, the ordination of LGBTQ folks had been allowed in our denomination for only a year and still rarely occurred. Many of us came from communities and churches where being open about our identities was still a huge risk. Most of us knew people who couldn't bear the thought of anyone like us becoming a pastor, whether from genuine religious conviction or fear or simple prejudice. I was a year into identifying as queer and still not yet fully out to my family or the wider world. The retreat was an equal parts jarring and comforting experience, secretly being only a couple hours north of my family, running around in the same ancient mountains where I'd attended summer camps as a child.

For three days, we had large-group sessions on leadership development, on professionalism, on owning and understanding your strengths. At the beginning of each day, we were invited to introduce ourselves and share our pronouns and any identifiers we wanted to name. We did this newly every morning—a somewhat uncommon practice—in recognition that who we are and who we understand ourselves to be can grow and evolve. I remember feeling so liberated by that idea, as though I could feel myself unfolding in the freedom of knowing I didn't have to have it all figured out just yet, or ever.

We had smaller groups too, in which we shared some of our more personal struggles and our hopes. In the evenings we had worship, where we led each other in prayers and songs that many of us had known since childhood and dreamed of the possibility that we might one day lead churches in the same way. At night, some of us gathered in the large room and piled together on the plethora of floor pillows. We laughed, swapped stories, shared secrets, and stayed up entirely too late, getting to know each other in the deep and intense way that can happen only in such contexts.

It was an imperfect but holy, precious space, made all the more so by the sense that in the world beyond there was nowhere quite as safe. Nowhere else that we could just be and be seen and known and trust that we would be loved as we were. There was a lot of crying and storytelling and anger and hope and fear. And community. And faith.

The focus that year was on learning to tell our stories to help bring about change in the church. We wrote "elevator speech" versions of our own stories of being LGBTQ and called to ministry, and we practiced them with each other. Our microtestimonies were offerings to each other, to our community, to ourselves and the church, and above all to God. I remember both the feeling of power and the absolute terror that came when I thought of telling my story to the world.

At worship the first night, Scott Clark, the dean of students from another Presbyterian seminary, offered a sermon on Hannah. He was one of the first openly LGBTQ people to be ordained after the Presbyterian Church began allowing LGBTQ ordination, and as such his life and ministry had become a model and an education for many. The passage he'd been given to preach on was the first part of Hannah's story—the part where she is denied agency and social capital and power not only because she is a woman, but because she is childless. Whether for this reason or for her own hopes for motherhood, Hannah spends years praying for a child, to no avail. Her husband's other wife, Peninnah, has an abundance of children and loves to rub it in Hannah's face. And Hannah's husband, Elkanah, we are told, loves Hannah and asks her why he isn't enough for her. He doesn't quite get it.

So Hannah goes to the temple and cries out to God. Because she speaks without making a sound, the priest, Eli, thinks she's drunk. He rebukes her, but she pushes right back. Hannah stands up in the temple and faces Eli and tells him, "I have been pouring out my soul before the Lord. Do not regard your servant as a worthless woman, for I have been speaking out of my great anxiety and vexation all this time" (1 Sam. 1:15–16).

In his sermon, Scott told us that the power of this part of Hannah's story is that she stands up before God and the temple in her full truth, baring her soul, and it puts a face and a story to the issue. Eli can no longer pretend not to see Hannah's struggle. He cannot simply write off her anguish as drunkenness. And God sees too. "One day, Hannah stood up" was the refrain of Scott's sermon. He told us that the great potential and challenge of our lives and ministry are that when we, too, dare to stand before the church and world in our full truth—as both LGBTQ and called—we also personify the issue. When we are vulnerable and allow ourselves to be seen authentically, the church is compelled to see and feel and know us. And there is power in that.

At the end of his sermon, Scott urged us to go out into the world and stand in our full truth as beloved children of God. And he told us we were going to practice that night, together in solidarity and shared vulnerability. And so the last time he said, "One day, Hannah stood up," we all stood together. Looking each other in the eyes, nodding in honor and recognition of the power of our truths. It was one of the most powerfully transformative and vulnerable experiences of my entire life. I know I'm not alone in that. On the strength of that experience, I left that retreat and shortly thereafter came out to the world. When I did, I got a small tattoo of the word "Hannah" in Hebrew, so that I would always remember the power of standing up in my truth and allowing myself to be seen.

## Putting Vulnerability in Its Place
### (That Is, in the Church and the World)

Church, at its best, is a place where people can dare enough and trust enough to show up in their full truth, to be fully seen and known. Church is meant to be a holy space where our broken edges and messy selves are received and held and embraced. It is supposed to be a space where we learn to do that for others, even when it's uncomfortable and hard. Even when everything in the world outside the church tells us that such action is weakness and creates risk. In a perfect world, it would look like a holistic community with infinite edges, so defined by equity, justice, and trust that everyone felt free to be in mutual vulnerability with one another. Its example would topple worldly systems of exploitation and subjugation by infectious witness alone, and topple even its own border walls to spill out into the vast and hungry earth.

We don't live in a perfect world. Not even close. And painfully, church is often the last place where people feel that they can show up as themselves. We arrive to our so-called fellowship halls in our Sunday best both literally and figuratively. We small-talk our way through coffee hours with our handbags and small pockets, and if we dare to carry any of our baggage at all, we make sure it's shined up and closed tight. Then we go home to our messy lives—our unsanctioned love lives and addictions and illnesses and blemishes and family troubles and depression and desperate longing, and we wonder when or if our lonely, shame-filled isolation will ever end. But we have just left the very place we should have found its ending. We are starving, and the Table of God's banquet—where wholeness is born from brokenness—is the one place promised to quell our hunger. But we fence it and guard it behind notions of purity and perfection.

We can be better. We must be better. This world is hungry, too, for a vision of what "better" looks like, and these days, church is so rarely the place that offers that vision. I have seen it, though. I saw glimpses in my childhood church. I saw it in the mountains of North Georgia. I saw it at my seminary bar, for goodness' sake. We can be better. And when we are, the result is incredible, holy transformation.

What it requires of us is a willingness to acknowledge that we, as a whole, are not yet a safe space. It asks that we cultivate and support other spaces, sometimes utterly un-church-like spaces, that can be safe in ways that we cannot yet be. It demands that we honor the role played by affinity groups and communities of shared struggle, even if it means they're not places for us to participate in. And for those of us who have every reason to trust the powers that be, who have never or rarely been forced into vulnerable realities, it means a willingness to be vulnerable without expecting it from those who have had it forced on them elsewhere. And that vulnerability doesn't always look like sharing our deepest feelings and fears and insecurities—at least not with those who've been hurt by the very things we cling to for safety. Sometimes, in such contexts, vulnerability looks like quiet. Like listening. Like really awkward learning. Like leaning into the discomfort of acknowledging one truth and slowly, intentionally growing into a new one.

Sometimes faithfully living out the call to encourage and embrace vulnerability means decentering our own experiences entirely. If we've always (or nearly always) felt relatively safe being vulnerable—if it's always felt like a choice—cultivating that space for others means examining the differences in experience and privilege that allow for that disparity, and working to defy even the most subtle aspects of our church culture (and beyond!) that perpetuate such disparities. This can also look like showing up for others, taking on some risk to stand with those who've had risk and vulnerability inflicted on them. It looks like risking getting things wrong, and getting called out for it, and then trying again. When we're not used to the risks—when we've always had a choice not to risk—it can be overwhelming. But it's important.

Above all, building a world that honors and benefits from vulnerability means doing something incredibly vulnerable in its own right: giving up control of the outcome. We open ourselves; we risk showing up in our own truth, authentic and vulnerable; and we honor and receive the vulnerability of others. And then we wait, with hopeful expectation, to see how everything, *everything*, is utterly transformed.

*Chapter Seven*

# The Gift of Trouble

Sometime in high school, I was given an album of the Beatles' greatest hits, which launched me into something of a Beatles phase. Fitting my personality, I had a particular fondness for their slow, sad songs: "Eleanor Rigby," "Yesterday," "Hey Jude." And then there was "Let It Be"—a song that somehow or another always seemed to speak into the moment. At that point in my life, I could hardly conceive of a God who was anything other than thoroughly male, but I found comfort in the sense of a sort of divine motherly presence who, whenever things seemed particularly dark, could be felt nearby.

A few years after that, the movie *Across the Universe* came out. It was part of a trend of movie musicals at the time, and it sought to bring the Beatles' music to life by constructing an intertwined anthology of stories about the turbulent 1960s, all to the tune of some of the Beatles' most loved songs. In one early part, a lone young voice begins to sing "Let It Be." On-screen, a main character learns that her young boyfriend has died in Vietnam, and then the image switches to the young black boy who is singing the song. He is hiding behind the shell of a car that is still on fire, and all around him the 1967 Detroit riot rages on. As black men are gunned down by police in riot gear, the boy sings, "When I find myself in times of trouble, Mother Mary comes to me, speaking words of wisdom: Let it be." The boy's voice gives way to a full church choir that belts out the chorus of the song while the scenes change again, switching back and forth between two funerals. One is for the soldier killed in the war, and the other for someone killed in the riot. Toward the end of the song, the young boy picks up the solo again, and only then are we shown who lies in the casket. It is the boy himself who has been killed.

I watched this scene unfold with heavy sobs aching my chest, and my understanding of that song changed forever. I had always heard it as a word of comfort and an invitation to let go of the heavy things that trouble me. But watching a young black boy sing the song in the midst of a scene of ongoing and deadly violence, I heard a new message in the words—to let the trouble be. To see it for what it is, feel the pain of it in my chest, and not hide from what troubles and discomforts me.

Revisiting these lyrics and that movie scene all these years later, after the deaths of Trayvon Martin, Mike Brown, Tamir Rice, Sandra Bland, and so many others, they carry an even greater weight. In this season of so much violence and hatred and division, there is such temptation to hide, to look away, to block out the overwhelming bad that makes our stomachs turn and our hearts ache. But I am more and more convinced that the answer—whatever it is—won't be found by turning away from what troubles us, but rather by finally and fully facing it.

## The Trouble with Trouble
### (How Trouble Separates Us)

When I was nineteen, I spent a summer in Chimaltenengo, Guatemala, volunteering for an environmental nonprofit and staying with the family of one of its employees. There was much about that experience that challenged me and opened my eyes in new ways. But perhaps the most striking lesson was the realization that I'd been taught to avoid the uncomfortable—that I'd grown up learning to see the troubling as profane and in need of being censored.

One evening of my time there, I sat in the living room with my host family watching the news. There had been a massive mudslide in the northern part of the country. It was a horrific tragedy with a significant death toll. I could only just follow the newscaster's words in Spanish, but the images on-screen spoke for themselves. The camera panned over body after body, revealing the mounting number of victims. The positions the bodies were in, the lifeless faces of adults and children, painted a gut-wrenching story. I remember the feeling of shock at seeing those bodies on television. It felt like cold seeping into my chest, where my heart was drumming at an increasingly high rate. I looked to my host family to see if they shared my shock, but their faces showed only sorrow.

I had never seen a dead body on the news. In America— particularly in my suburban context—the closest our news reports got to showing the magnitude of a tragedy was lots of flashing lights and police tape, crying survivors offering testimony, and perhaps a smiling still photograph of a victim. These things have their own power, of course, and their own way of telling a story. But that news report in Guatemala made me realize how much more deeply I was impacted by seeing the genuine reality of what had taken place.

Sometime after that, I was visiting one of the villages we worked in, Como Lapa. It was known for being an artists' village. All along the main street through the town, there was a wall with a mural painted on it. It told the entire history of the village, including a violent massacre that occurred during a government overthrow and an earthquake that devastated the people. Again, I was unsettled by a portrait of so much pain being the dominant visual for the town. But talking with the people, I began to understand: this was part of their story, and it deserved to be fully seen and felt and understood.

In general, I have found that our instinctive response to what troubles us is to avoid it. We do not like being uncomfortable—it feels threatening. And so we sanitize stories, we censor people, and we avoid spaces and topics that are deemed too troubling. Unfortunately, in our rush to put distance between ourselves and what troubles us, we end up putting distance between ourselves and other people whose realities make us uncomfortable. By refusing to see the full scope of their story, we also fail to fully see them. Removed as we become from others in our efforts to remain untroubled, we excuse away their pain and divest ourselves of any power we might have to change things. Our understandings of what is real and true grow further and further apart from one another, and divisions become more and more entrenched.

The church has played no small role in this avoidance. On the one hand, the church claims to serve others in the name of Christ. It purports to be a space where all people can bring their own broken selves and be seen and received for who they are. But far too often, in our efforts to make sure that people who sit in our pews are comfortable (and will keep coming back), we refrain from preaching on controversial topics or else face criticism for "putting politics in the pulpit." We send mission teams out into the world to serve, but treat the trips like tourism and privilege our people's experience over the actual needs and impact of those we seek to serve. By avoiding exposure to anything too troubling, be it a controversial issue or the harshness of suffering, we are almost always choosing some people's comfort over others, and more often than not, the people whose comfort we sacrifice are those who are unlikely to find comfort beyond our walls either.

The phrase "comfort the afflicted and afflict the comfortable" was originally intended to describe the work of journalism, but over the last few decades it has been popularly applied to the work of God and the church.[1] It offers a challenge to the way we understand the church's role. If we truly intend the church to be a place where all are welcome and an institution that strives to do the work of Jesus Christ in service to others, then we must relinquish our expectation that we should always be comfortable in church. If we believe, as we claim, that God despises sin and seeks to heal what is broken, then we absolutely should not settle for comfort in the face of such a broken world.

What if, instead, those who find comfort nowhere else could find it in the church, and those who've grown to count on comfort at the expense of fully seeing the brokenness of this world were encouraged to face their own discomfort? To sit with it and discern what truths that discomfort speaks surrounded by a community of love? What if the church became a place where we were all welcomed into confronting that which troubles us and that which should trouble us? And then, having seen the painful truth, might we finally be able to hear what God is calling us to do about it?

It cannot be considered political and improper to name the pain and horrors of this world. We must name them, if we would ever truly seek to change them. Our discomfort carries a message. That which troubles us seeks to tell us the truth. Will we learn to listen?

## The Troublemaker and the Trouble-Embracers
### (Trouble in the Bible)

"Do not let your hearts be troubled," John 14 tells us, reassuring us that God's house has many dwelling places for those who have faith. Elsewhere, in the Gospel according to Matthew, we are firmly instructed to "consider the lilies of the field," and ask ourselves, "Can any of you by worrying add a single hour to your span of life?" (Matt. 6:27–28). These may be the most recognizable biblical references to worry and trouble, but they hardly paint a full picture of how Jesus calls upon us to engage with that which is troubling.

From the very beginning, Jesus is not only disinterested in trying to avoid trouble, he is—in fact—a *troublemaker*. Several chapters before the lesson of lilies and worrying, Matthew recounts the events that follow the birth of Christ (Matt. 2:1–12). As he tells it, Jesus is born in Judea during the time of King Herod, and when wise men from the East come searching for the child, King Herod freaks out a little bit. It's worth noting that King Herod isn't the only one frightened to hear that a newborn child has been "born king of the Jews." Matthew tells us that "all Jerusalem" is frightened with him.

The word translated in the NRSV as "frightened"—translated elsewhere as "troubled"—is a form of the Greek word *tarassō*. Its meaning is described as "to stir up that which needs to remain still."[2] This is the reaction that Jesus causes in power, principalities, and the everyday citizens of Jerusalem from the moment of his birth. This word—*tarassō*—follows Jesus too. It's the same word used to describe Zechariah's reaction when an angel brings news of John's impending birth (Luke 1:12). It's also the word used to describe how the disciples feel when they see Jesus walking on water (Matt. 14:26; Mark 6:50). They are his loyal followers; they have seen him perform many miracles. But when he walks on the water toward them, they are not calmed or even impressed. They are troubled. They know something big is stirring up.

Jesus comes into the world to challenge the status quo, to take hold of the things we so desperately need to remain in place in order to maintain our sense of security and comfort—and he throws that out the window. Jesus comes to cause a whole lot of holy trouble, and he does it in the name of truth. The promise of Jesus is not just peace, it's a peace that follows only after massive and irrevocable upheaval.

I'll admit, I relate to Herod and the people of Jerusalem much more than I wish I did. I am a person who likes to be in control. I don't mind the unexpected, as long as it's within reason and I'm given time to adjust and it doesn't push me too far. Which is to say, I guess I do mind the unexpected. Truthfully, I don't know many people who would claim to love trouble—whether it's the positive world-changing kind Jesus brings, or the devastating world-challenging kind that fills our news feeds and television screens these days.

Still, recognizing that Jesus himself comes into this very troubled world to stir up trouble of his own makes me wonder if maybe there isn't a choice between trouble or no trouble. Maybe the troubles of this world must be faced and reckoned with, and maybe they can only be overcome by the good and holy trouble Jesus exemplifies.

Herod and the Jerusalemites, and I on my less courageous days, may choose to cower in the face of trouble, but the magi make a different choice. They have seen a rising star and followed it in search of a newborn king to a people not their own. By all accounts, Jesus is not their messiah, not their story, but still they travel a long, hard road to seek him out. And in their journeying, they come upon a frightened and frightening king who commands that they return to him with information on the young boy's whereabouts so that he "might pay him homage." When the three magi finally find themselves standing in the doorway of the Son of God, they bow before him and offer gifts. And then, rather than return to Herod, they choose to go home another way. We don't know what becomes of them after this. We don't know if they make it home without harm or make it home at all. But what we know of them is that, where Herod sought to avoid the trouble Jesus was bringing, the magi face risk and danger and worldly trouble of all kinds in order to embrace the holy trouble of God. They choose to recognize and be utterly changed by the truth.

During the summer of 2015, I was scheduled to preach the Sunday after a white-supremacist young man opened fire inside an AME church in Charleston, South Carolina, and killed nine people at a Bible study. Most of my more senior colleagues were out of town, and I was left to wrestle some meaningful message of that week's lectionary text, which was the story of Jesus asleep in the boat when a storm comes upon the disciples on the Sea of Galilee (Mark 4:35–41). We generally describe this story as "Jesus calming the storm," but I was struck, in that particular horror-drenched week, by how long Jesus stays asleep. A massive storm is raging. His closest followers are crying out, in fear for their lives, and he sleeps soundly, apparently untroubled. When he finally wakes up and calms the raging winds with a word, he then turns to his disciples and scolds them, saying, "Why are you afraid? Have you still no faith?"

I confess that I may have a higher-than-average propensity for getting annoyed with Jesus. I don't love him any less, nor am I any less committed to his teachings on the whole. But I also believe strongly in his humanity, and for me it shows up sometimes in his tendency to snap at people when things don't go according to plan. Reading about the sleeping Messiah in a week that felt so fully like the world was on fire, I was not just annoyed with Jesus. I was angry. In my struggles with this passage, it felt to me like Jesus was the one refusing to bear witness to the trouble all around him. I was furious at the notion of a Savior who would willingly disengage and then rebuke those calling on him for their faithlessness.

It was also impossible, in that week, to read about a sleeping Christ and not think about the little girl who survived the massacre at Emanuel AME Church by playing dead on the floor among the bodies of those she loved so the shooter wouldn't notice her. Her grandmother had taught her to do that. The Charleston massacre was a shock to my system—a horrific act of violence that I could scarcely imagine before it was real. But here was a little girl, a baby really, who knew enough of the troubles of the world to recognize that she should play dead in the midst of a massacre. It became abundantly clear for me, as I thought about that child, that some of us have much more ability to sleep through and ignore what troubles us than others. Not everyone has that luxury.

I couldn't reconcile the notion of a Savior who would sleep in the face of terrifying trouble with a world in which little girls learn how to survive a shooting before they learn to read—a world which he came to save. And so I began to ask questions of this story. I began to wonder what our storm is—what trouble is raging all around us. In those days and even now, the obvious answer seems to be violence, bigotry, hate, white supremacy, and so much more. But a wise friend challenged me to consider that these troubles couldn't be our storm—they've been around since forever. They are so much a part of our reality that we have mostly lost the ability to even recognize them, let alone fully confront them. They are the water we swim in. Perhaps, my friend suggested, the storm that rages on is one of demands for justice and protest and holy unrest that stir up the water all around us.

If this is the case, then maybe Jesus isn't so oblivious to the storm after all. Maybe when Jesus scolds his disciples, it isn't because he cannot empathize with their fear, but because they are afraid of the wrong thing. It seems to me that Jesus waited to calm the storm because, sometimes, some storms need to rage. In fact, looking at this story through the lens of our modern reality—I don't think Jesus is the one asleep at all. I think we are. Those of us with the freedom and privilege and luxury of complacency in the face of all that is evil in this world. The lesson of this story—much like the Beatles' song—isn't that we shouldn't be concerned by the trouble all around us. It's that we *should* be. We cannot claim to be faithful and expect to be sheltered from the troubles of the world. We must recognize them, and recognize the righteous storms that rise up in response. We are called to hear those deeply painful and uncomfortable truths that trouble our hearts and roil our guts—those that we would sooner have calmed or be swept away from. We are called to be stirred up in response, to become the storm itself.

The troubles of this broken world are never a blessing, but the storms that rise up around us and within us in response to that brokenness—those are good and holy trouble. And however long we choose to look away in the face of what troubles us, God will allow those righteous storms to rage.

As I finally found the words to say, in the wake of Dylann Roof's violent destruction, "God's faithfulness both endures and rejects our demand for comfort. God's love doesn't quell our fears but asks us why we cower in fear when there is work to be done. In unswerving, steadfast, indomitable love for us, God lets the holy storm of protest and justice rage on. Until we wake up. Until we wake up."[3]

## In Trouble, *Veritas*
### (How Trouble Saves Us)

The God who lets righteous storms rage and speaks in both silence and the whirlwind shows us that there is a gift to be dis-covered in that which troubles us. Or at least, in our capacity to be troubled. That gnawing feeling inside us, the cold snap of horrific realization in our chest, the compulsion to stay and watch when every instinct inside us is screaming to look away and avoid and forget—that feeling of being troubled gives us truth. And it is a truth that we must see and acknowledge and feel fully before we can ever really respond to it or transform it.

We are troubled because we should be. We are troubled because there are truths we must confront and respond to and overthrow. We are troubled because, even though sometimes it feels like it, we are not yet fully lost. When we allow ourselves to feel the weight of our troubledness, we bear witness to the truth.

All those years ago in Guatemala, one afternoon I visited a village with the employee who was hosting me for the summer. We made our rounds to village members who helped run the nursery we had started. We checked on their efforts to make agroforestry work against the devastation that deforestation had brought upon them. On our way home, we made a final stop at the very edge of the village. In a tiny shack was a woman who looked older than anyone I'd ever met. She sat on the ground beside a fire in the center of her home, without a chimney to funnel out the smoke. We gathered near her, ducking beneath the smoke. My colleague greeted her and spoke to her in Spanish, and I did my best to follow along.

Before long, she began to speak slowly but passionately. She wept as she spoke, her words as much moaning as anything else. She told us that no one came to see her anymore. That she spent her days alone and sad, waiting to die. And she said that there were worse things than dying. It was worse to be forgotten, as she had been. She asked that we remember her.

Even as I struggled to understand her with my rudimentary Spanish, I was overcome by the depth of her pain. At nineteen, I couldn't fathom what it felt like to grow old, to lose your spouse, your peers and friends, and then to be forgotten or left behind by your children and grandchildren. Her daughter lived not far from her, in the middle of the village—she was one of the ones who had greeted us warmly earlier in the day and offered us homemade tortillas. I wasn't sure if it was really true that she never came to see her mother, but it was clear that this woman's pain and loneliness were real. I felt so powerless against them that I wanted to rationalize it away or forget it, but she had asked me to promise to remember, and so I did.

Everyone deserves to be seen and remembered. Even the hardest truths must be borne witness to. These days, there is no shortage of troubling truth out there. There are Syrian toddlers drowning as they flee a war-demolished home, and other children torn from their families as they seek to cross the border. There are transgender people—especially women of color—murdered every week, and efforts are under way to define gender in a way that denies their very existence. Young black men and women are still being shot down, often by representatives of the very institutions we are expected to trust. In late 2018, five police officers were shot in my father's hometown, and one young female officer eventually died after weeks of fighting for her life. Around the same time, a right-wing extremist mailed pipe bombs to more than a dozen Democratic politicians, news agencies, and other public figures. And in the same month, a man opened fire in a Pittsburgh synagogue during morning Shabbat services and killed eleven people in what was described as the worst act of anti-Semitic violence in US history.

The acceptable reaction to such tragedies in today's world from both leaders and everyday people is to offer our "thoughts and prayers"—to voice on social media and in public our unity and solidarity with those directly affected. Then, after a moment or two of reflection, we move on with our lives until the next horrible thing happens. We aren't supposed to dig into the troubling realities or address the deep, underlying injustices that allow these terrible things to happen. We can offer our thoughts and prayers, but we can't offer our outrage at the way others and even we ourselves are complicit. That is too divisive, too political, too troubling.

There is so much in this world to be troubled by, and we are becoming worse and worse at being troubled by any of it, every single day. We cannot lose our capacity to be horrified. Faithfulness requires that we bear witness not just as we scroll past the story. Bearing witness means that we feel the weight of hard truth.

In Brooklyn, New York, there is an old church building that clearly once belonged to a large and thriving congregation. These days, that building is occupied by a smaller family of believers on Sunday mornings, though their congregation is just as full of life. They are called the Church of Gethsemane, and they have a unique ministry. Many of their members do not step through the doors of their sanctuary for years, and yet their voices help shape the church's worship. Founded in 1986 as a worshiping community, and as a church in 1989, the Church of Gethsemane is a Presbyterian congregation whose focus is incarcerated and previously incarcerated people, as well as their families and loved ones. They keep a membership of those currently incarcerated and communicate with them regularly via letters. Every week they read a selection of letters from their incarcerated members during worship as part of the response to the Word. This community recognizes that God has sat with many in prisons, and that those who are incarcerated have stories that matter too. Their stories are often hard to hear—troubling—but Gethsemane sees God speaking truth through them. Gethsemane knows that those truths deserve to be seen and known and felt.

### Embracing the Gifts of Trouble

Recognizing there are gifts to be found in what troubles us, recognizing that there is such a thing as holy trouble, does not mean to suggest that the very troubling things that happen in this world occur by divine design or that we are meant to view the horrors themselves as gifts. The gift is born less from the trouble than from the feeling of being troubled—which is a reminder of both our humanity and our connectedness, and the truth that trouble can reveal to us when we learn to sit in our discomfort and reckon with it.

It's also important to note that there is a balance to this work. While it is important not to hide from or avoid the troubling realities that our faith calls us to confront, it's also true that some people and communities don't have the choice to hide, and we should not exacerbate their trouble. They are inundated with troubling realities, with horrific scenes, with devastating loss. Sometimes, in our efforts to effectively capture the full scope of something terrible, we end up forcing traumatic images and stories on people who are already traumatized enough. Meanwhile, those of us who feel more removed from such trauma can actually become *more* desensitized by the oversaturation of horrific imagery and details about deeply traumatic realities experienced by other people.

In a piece for the *Sojourners'* website, Jamar A. Boyd names the ubiquitous—inescapable, really—presence of the murder of black people in our news, and observes, "The brutal lethargy of Americans to the plight of black and brown citizens is a bleeding wound without a bandage large enough to heal it. And yet, America still doesn't give a damn."[4]

In 2016, *PBS NewsHour* reported that when videos of black people being killed go viral on the internet, seeing the imagery over and over can cause PTSD-like symptoms in other black people.[5] The article quotes Monnica Williams, a clinical psychologist. "It's upsetting and stressful for people of color to see these events unfolding," she says. "It can lead to depression, substance abuse, and in some cases, psychosis. Very often, it can contribute to health problems that are already common among African-Americans such as high blood pressure."

The same year, Maureen Callahan wrote a piece for the *New York Post* about Hollywood's obsession with black pain, pointing out, "There's a seeming cynicism in Hollywood's endless revisiting of slavery narratives, and the films are almost always released during awards season, with a disturbing subtext: How great and liberal are we, these powerful, rich, white people, taking responsibility for this atrocity over and over?"[6] In the same article, director Justin Simien says, "If you see a black movie, it's typically historical, and it tends to deal with our pain. You know what that says, very subtly? It says that we're not human. Because human beings are multifaceted." Exploring the same idea in a piece called "Decolonizing Empathy: Why Our Pain Will Never Be Enough to Disarm White Supremacy," Sherronda J. Brown writes, "Our ability to recognize pain in others is at the core of our ability to feel empathy. If non-white people do not feel or react to pain in the same way as white people in the white imagination, then that affects how white empathy for others is formed, or whether it is informed at all."[7]

We do have a responsibility to acknowledge and reckon with the things that trouble us, and we do have a responsibility to be troubled by the horrors of this world. Sometimes, those of us who encounter these things from a distance need to be exposed to the pain experienced by the people involved and connected to tragedies, violent realities, and other terrible things. But as we do that important work, we also must continually ask whether the development of empathy, the recognition of troubling truth for the purpose of responding to it, is our true aim or if we've wandered off into some other motivation: fascination, entertainment, fetishization. In short, we must be attentive and intentional.

When we are, confronting what troubles us can be a powerful motivator for change, for honoring truth by no longer avoiding it, for bearing witness, and for remembering that we are all bound up together. As the church, as people of faith, we are called to bear witness. And that calling is not witnessing just to the good of this world, but also to its brokenness, to its evils, and to its people's pain. There is holiness in being present to these truths. And then having seen them for what they are, having been deeply troubled by them—we deepen our resolve to work for better, and join in the long, slow effort toward both healing and justice.

*Chapter Eight*

# The Gift of Protest

In Beijing, China, in 1989, protests raged from mid-April to early June.[1] The movement was led by students calling for a more democratic government. In an effort to suppress the protests, Premier Li Peng declared martial law. After several months of protests alongside attempts to enforce the martial law, the clash came to a violent head on June 4 in Tiananmen Square, when thousands of troops from the People's Liberation Army used automatic weapons, snipers, and tanks to forcibly disperse the gathered protesters. China has said that the number of youth killed wasn't more than three hundred, though others have claimed the death toll was higher than ten thousand. The bodies were cleared away and incinerated, the blood hosed into the gutters. To this day, many consider it to be one of the bloodiest and most horrific events in modern history.

The next day, a few foreign photojournalists captured an iconic moment. A single man, wearing a white collared shirt and holding two shopping bags, stood alone in front of a line of hulking tanks, blocking their path out of Tiananmen Square. As the tanks shifted to circumvent the man, he shifted too, temporarily halting them. Though for years the man was unknown, a June 2018 article in the *Independent* claims that he was eventually identified as a nineteen-year-old archaeology student named Wang Weilin. It is not known what happened to him after his solitary protest, but the image of his small frame holding back the tide of massive tanks has become one of the most iconic protest images of all time.

Other protests have also created powerful images. A photograph from 1967 in the United States shows a young man protesting the Vietnam War by placing a carnation in the barrel of a rifle held by a soldier, a demonstration of "flower power," a term describing the peaceful protest movements of the 1960s. There was the horrifying television coverage of civil rights protesters being beaten on Selma's Bloody Sunday in 1965, followed by the iconic image of protesters defiantly linking arms when the march finally successfully happened weeks later. More recently, in the midst of growing protests against the Confederate flags flown in front of government buildings in the South, young activist Bree Newsome scaled the flagpole in front of the South Carolina capitol in Columbia and took down the Confederate flag that still hung there. Photographers captured the image of her, in full harness and climbing gear, holding out the flag from the top of the pole after she had removed it.

These moments in history, captured in striking, perfectly timed video footage and photographs, become indelibly impressed in our memories. They become icons, symbols of the power of the human spirit and the value of standing up for what we believe in. They embody the sentiment expressed in that ubiquitous class-room poster: "What is popular is not always right, and what is right is not always popular." Immortalized in these images, the people they depict become no longer "protesters" but "freedom fighters" and even modern-day "saints."

Of course, in actuality, we almost never treat them with that degree of reverence or respect in the moment. At least, not as a whole. In the moment, a single protester isn't a "freedom fighter" or "saint," but rather an "agitator." A collection of protesters is nothing so harmless as a "group," and even if they're lucky enough to be called a "demonstration," it doesn't take much before they're labeled a "riot." Society rebukes them for disrupt-ing the status quo. We say they should use the proper channels to air their grievances; we ignore that peaceful protest is legal, at least in the United States. We claim the very act of protesting is violent, and on that basis, that the concerns they raise don't deserve to be heard. We arrest them, punish them, and do what we can to silence them. Sometimes, we even kill them.

From the safe distance of history, we either dismiss them entirely, or we armchair-quarterback their methodology, their contradictions, their failures. Or else we canonize them, refuse to reckon with their full, imperfect humanity. We turn them into something more than human, co-opt their legacy, and turn their provocative messages into something a little more palatable— worthy of an inspirational poster, or perhaps a sermon quote that will score us points without rocking the boat . . . too much.

In theory we love protesters, but in practice, we rarely love them well. Protest stirs things up. It draws hard lines. It gives voice and visibility to dissent and division that we would prefer to ignore or deal with more quietly. Protest functions as an inescapable mirror of truth, reflecting back to us how often the unity we idealize is a hollow illusion that requires silent suffering and injustice to persist. Protest reminds us that without justice, there is no peace. There is a gift to be found in justice-seeking, change-seeking protest—not just for the protester, but for all of us. But often, we are too busy trying to contain the uprising to receive it. And that makes me wonder if we really deserve it at all.

## Protest and the Church: Frenemies for Life
### (How Protest Separates Us)

The church is no stranger to protest. At various points, they have walked hand in hand. Few have had their faith associated with their defiance and protest more overtly than Dietrich Bonhoeffer.[2] Born in 1906 in a German city that is now a part of Poland, Bonhoeffer grew up around the dialogues and priorities of academia with a father who worked as a professor of psychiatry and neurology at the University of Berlin. Among other things, the senior Bonhoeffer was known as an early opponent of Hitler's T4 program, an initiative that called for killing (euphemistically referred to as "euthanasia") the elderly, those with mental or physical disabilities, and those who suffered from illnesses that had no cure.[3]

Dietrich Bonhoeffer went into academic study himself, pursuing studies in theology at both the University of Tübingen and Berlin during the mid-1920s. After a stint as pastor to a German-speaking congregation in Spain and a year of study in America, Bonhoeffer returned to Berlin to teach theology at the university. When the Nazi regime arose in the early 1930s, Bonhoeffer vehemently and publicly opposed it, and became a leader in the Confessing Church movement, which was the primary anti-Nazi resistance movement of German Protestantism. The primary focus of Bonhoeffer's objections was the oppression of practicing Christians with Jewish ancestry, as opposed to practicing Jews. Still, he spent the rest of his life vocally protesting and fighting against Nazism. Though he briefly sought refuge in the United States in 1939, he returned to Germany after only two weeks, resolved to continue his resistance work. He was eventually imprisoned and later was discovered to have been a part of a conspiracy assassination attempt against Hitler.

For Bonhoeffer, his faith was a primary impetus for his protest, compelling his belief that "we are not to simply bandage the wounds of victims beneath the wheels of injustice, we are to drive a spoke into the wheel itself."[4] Bonhoeffer neither believed in nor practiced a polite, subtle, or passive resistance. He believed that "there is no way to peace along the way to safety. For peace must be dared. It is the great venture."[5] One of the theologians he most respected and followed was Karl Barth, who also protested against the Nazi regime as part of the Confessing Church movement, and became the primary author of the Barmen Declaration, which was adopted by Christians in Germany who opposed both Nazism and the church's participation in it.[6]

This last point speaks to a crucial truth about the church's relationship to protest. While certainly, theologians and faith leaders like Bonhoeffer, Barth, and countless others made vehement protest against injustice and evil in the name of their faith, the institutional church was often complicit in the very evils being protested against—the German Christian Church being only one example. Like Barth, Bonhoeffer levied intense criticism against the faithlessness of a complicit Christianity.

In a sermon given to a congregation in London where he served for eighteen months in the midst of the Nazi occupation of Europe,[7] Bonhoeffer said, "Christianity stands or falls with its revolutionary protest against violence, arbitrariness, and pride of power, and with its plea for the weak. Christians are doing too little to make these points clear. . . . Christendom adjusts itself far too easily to the worship of power. Christians should give more offense, shock the world far more, than they are doing now."[8] In a letter to Erwin Sutz in 1934, Bonhoeffer had this to say about silence in the church: "We must finally stop appealing to theology to justify our reserved silence about what the state is doing—for that is nothing but fear. 'Open your mouth for the one who is voiceless'—for who in the church today still remembers that that is the least of the Bible's demands in times such as these?"[9]

In America, not too many years after Bonhoeffer's death, Christian pastors and faith leaders were once again fighting hate and systemic injustice in the name of their faith. One of the most famous among them, no doubt, was the Rev. Dr. Martin Luther King Jr., born in 1929 to a Baptist pastor father and a former schoolteacher mother.[10] He would be the third generation in his family to serve as pastor at Ebenezer Baptist Church in Atlanta, after his grandfather and father. By age twenty-four, King had received a doctorate in systematic theology from Boston University and begun to pastor a church in Montgomery, Alabama. Not even a year later, Montgomery became the focal point of the US civil rights movement when Rosa Parks refused to give up her seat on the bus and the Montgomery bus boycott was launched. Martin Luther King became the leader and spokesperson for that protest movement, and subsequently one of the most prominent activists in the civil rights movement.

King, along with other ministers and activists, founded the Southern Christian Leadership Conference in 1957, of which he served as president. Eventually, King moved to Atlanta and took a co-pastorate with his father at Ebenezer, all the while continuing his work for justice for black Americans. The key tactics of his protest efforts were nonviolent resistance and civil disobedience, drawing inspiration from the protest work of Mahatma Gandhi. Along with Gandhi, King also credited gay black activist Bayard Rustin and King's own Christian faith as the inspiration for his efforts. Despite the peaceful nature of King's protests, he faced threats from individuals and institutions alike. His home was firebombed in the wake of the Montgomery bus boycott, and he was arrested twenty-nine separate times.[11] Eventually, in 1968, he was assassinated by a sniper the day after giving his famous "I Have Been to the Mountaintop" speech in Memphis, Tennessee. He was thirty-nine years old.

Though King credited his own Christian faith as a primary motivator of his ceaseless efforts toward justice, he, like Bonhoeffer and Barth before him, had hard words for the complacency and complicity of the church—particularly white moderate churches. In his "Letter from Birmingham Jail" King made the argument, "One has not only a legal but a moral responsibility to obey just laws. Conversely, one has a moral responsibility to disobey unjust laws." He offered a passionate critique of white moderates, saying,

> I must confess that over the past few years I have been gravely disappointed with the white moderate. I have almost reached the regrettable conclusion that the Negro's great stumbling block in his stride toward freedom is not the White Citizen's Counciler or the Ku Klux Klanner, but the white moderate, who is more devoted to "order" than to justice; who prefers a negative peace which is the absence of tension to a positive peace which is the presence of justice; who constantly says: "I agree with you in the goal you seek, but I cannot agree with your methods of direct action"; who paternalistically believes he can set the timetable for another man's freedom; who lives by a mythical concept of time and who constantly advises the Negro to wait for a "more convenient season." Shallow understanding from people of good will is more frustrating than absolute misunderstanding

from people of ill will. Lukewarm acceptance is much more bewildering than outright rejection.[12]

For King, as for so many others, faithfulness did not amount to silent acquiescence. In the same breath in which he rejects complacency and a failure to protest, he also calls out the dangerous way that avoidance of tension, as discussed earlier in this book, can subvert justice. These things were, to King, deeply connected, and to avoid tension and fail to protest in the absence of justice was to fail one's commitment to God and God's Beloved Community.

King's letter was written in response to a statement released by eight white Alabama clergymen on the day after King's arrest. Their statement rejected the civil rights demonstrations of King and others, saying, "Just as we formerly pointed out that 'hatred and violence have no sanction in our religious and political traditions,' we also point out that such actions as incite to hatred and violence, however technically peaceful those actions may be, have not contributed to the resolution of our local problems. . . . When rights are consistently denied, a cause should be pressed in the courts and in negotiations among local leaders, and not in the streets."[13]

Today, King is beloved and oft-quoted in white and African American churches alike. And yet, this attitude expressed by the moderate white clergymen of King's time still persists. In the name of peace and civility, people are urged to go through "the proper channels" to achieve needed change, working within the system that exists rather than threatening it. Again and again, protest is written off as uncivil and disruptive, and its grasp for a positive peace that brings justice is forsaken for the relative convenience of a negative peace that maintains order.

## Holy Protest in the Bible

As in the case of argument, we have a tendency to gloss over protest when it shows up in the Bible, or otherwise emphasize instances where protests against God or Jesus were shown to be the indicators of an immature faith, as in the case of Peter's refusal to have his feet washed by Jesus. But a closer look—especially at those texts we spend less time on—reveals that protest has its own power.

In the book of Esther, a young Jewish woman more or less uses the king's affection for her to save her people, with the nudging and guidance of her uncle, Mordecai. Esther's story isn't one of protest, really. She works within the system and the role she's been given to achieve the justice she's seeking. But one of my favorite parts of Esther's story isn't about Esther at all, and it rarely gets any attention. In the first chapter of this short book, we meet King Ahasuerus, who is in only his third year of ruling an expansive kingdom. To show off his power and wealth, he invites officials from far and wide to partake in a banquet that lasts 180 days. And then, he throws an after-party. For seven days, he hosts a banquet for all the people of Susa, where he lives. And his wife, Queen Vashti, does her queenly duty by throwing a banquet for the women, who apparently don't count among the king's "all people of Susa."

On the last night, the king is drunk, and he calls for Queen Vashti to be brought to him so he might show her off to all the other men present. Scholars say there's some clear innuendo here. Even if we don't know the specifics of the king's intentions, we know he wasn't showing her off for her intelligence. He was showing off her beauty and her body, to an end we can only guess at. But Queen Vashti refuses to come. She has fulfilled her role dutifully up to this point, but she is absolutely unwilling to be used by her drunk husband in this way. And so she says no. She protests.

The immediate cost of Vashti's protest is that she is deposed from her crown. The king's sage advisers tell him that other women will look to Vashti as a hero and will join her in rebelling against their husbands' commands. And since that surely can't be allowed, Vashti is exiled and commanded to never come before King Ahasuerus again. The search begins for a new queen, and Esther steps into the spotlight.

We don't know what becomes of Queen Vashti after this. In the Bible, she is a passing parenthetical. But she sees her own life and her own worth as more than that, and so she dares to defy the king, to risk her life and her safety, to protest against the injustice being done to her. And though it isn't her intention, her act of protest is what allows Esther to do what she needs to do. If Vashti had never said no to the king, he never would have said yes to Esther being his new queen, and he never would have said yes to her pleas for her people. Protest has power even if it does not win.

Other times, acts of protest and defiance are the only path to change. In the Gospel according to Mark, we hear the story of the hemorrhaging woman, who makes herself known to Jesus despite social protocol and the great displeasure of the crowd. Jesus is on the way to heal the young daughter of a synagogue leader (Mark 5:25–34). The girl is dying; Jesus has no time to be interrupted, no time to get distracted by some "lesser" need. But the hemorrhaging woman—whose name we never learn—knows that time will never be on her side. She has been bleeding for twelve years. Twelve years. Many women bleed, and though for them it is a natural cycle, in those days a woman's time of bleeding made them unclean. They were required to set themselves apart until their bleeding was done. But this woman's bleeding was never done. And in her culture, that meant that for more than a decade, she was seen as unclean and unfit for being seen or being a part of society. She was isolated from friends and family, ostracized. She had no safety, no resources, no dignity. And no healing.

When she gets word that Jesus is passing her way, she must think to herself, "What do I have to lose?" She knows that change will not come for her unless she demands it. She knows that quietly following social protocol will not save her. She doesn't have the privilege of waiting for a more convenient time. She must make herself inconvenient. And so, in an act of civil disobedience, defiance, and desperation, she breaks all social protocol and pushes her way through the crowd, unclean though she is. She dares to clutch the hem of Jesus' robe, yet another rule broken, and immediately, her bleeding stops. Jesus feels the power going out of him and he turns to face her. She and the others around them wait, no doubt, for his rebuke. But it never comes. "Your faith has made you well," he tells her. And so he names her act of protest, of disruption, a praiseworthy mark of faith.

We see an even more overt case of protest in Jesus' parable of the Persistent Widow. In Luke 18, Jesus tells his followers about a jerk judge who doesn't care about God or people or justice. But this woman, a widow, who has experienced some kind of injustice at the hands of an adversary (Jesus doesn't tell us the details), comes to the judge asking him to rule in her favor. The judge refuses, because he doesn't care, but the woman just keeps coming. She protests the injustice done to her, and she protests the judge's indifference, and she keeps protesting no matter how many times she loses. Eventually, the judge relents and gives her justice, not because her protests have made him care, but because they have made her impossible to ignore. Jesus compares this woman's persistent protest to faithful prayer, and in so doing, he names it as holy.

## The Woman Who Looked Back
### (Protest against God)

Another woman who might well have known the power and necessity of protest is Lot's wife, whom Jewish teachings sometimes identify as Idit. My first year in seminary, I was invited by several senior students to help lead a "silenced voices" chapel service on campus, highlighting the stories of biblical women whose voices are never heard in Scripture, and I felt compelled to write about her. Her story has stuck with me ever since.

Idit is most recognized and remembered for foolishly disobeying her husband's command to not look back at the destruction of Sodom, and her subsequent punishment for disobedience: being turned into a pillar of salt. What a way to be remembered. But over time I've come to recognize her decision in that moment as a beautiful and powerful act of defiant protest against injustice and even God, for which she was willing to pay in both her life and her legacy.

Given tradition, Idit was likely young when she was married. She belonged to her husband entirely, and as he faithfully followed Abram (later Abraham) from Haran to famine-ravaged Canaan, to Egypt, to the Negeb, and finally to settle in Sodom, it was Idit's duty to faithfully follow her husband without question and without looking back. We don't know how she felt about all those moves and that hard nomadic life. We never hear her voice, perhaps in reflection of the fact that she was meant to quietly obey. In accordance with the expectation of her role, she bore Lot two children, daughters.

Then in Genesis 19, when guests came to their house in Sodom, and men from the city showed up at their door threatening to rape these guests, Lot offered his own daughters instead. And while Idit would no doubt have been horrified, she did not, as far as we know, intervene. What could she have done? Luckily, divine intervention spared them, and the guests—who, it turned out, were angels—blinded the mob of men so that Lot and his family could escape before God destroyed the city. The angels told Lot not to look back, and we might imagine him passing the same command on to his wife. Another direction she was expected to quietly obey. But she didn't obey. She looked back, and she was turned into a pillar of salt.

Tradition tells us that this act was foolish, but I imagine that Idit, in her final moments, found her courage and her voice. I imagine her life of silent obedience flashed through her mind, in service to her husband who had offered up her daughters like animals to slaughter and to a God who was at the very moment raining destruction and annihilation down upon her home and community. And I imagine that Idit decided that she had had enough of silent obedience. She looked back as one final desperate act of protest against a seemingly cruel God and a husband turned dangerous stranger. She became salt—a fitting monument to her tears and the pain they speak to. Idit was willing to die, but she wasn't willing to remain silent or acquiescent. She dared to protest against violent injustice, even when it seemed to come at the hands of God.

There are modern examples too. In the early 2000s, theologians Rebecca Ann Parker and Rita Nakashima Brock wrote a book called *Proverbs of Ashes*. In it, they speak from their experiences as

women, and more specifically, respectively, as a survivor of childhood sexual abuse and as an Asian woman reckoning with her
experiences of racial violence. From these vantage points, they
examine traditional Christian theologies of redemptive suffering,
divinely ordained violence, and the danger of abusive cross theology. They wrestle, through the lens of their own and others'
experiences, with the question of whether there is a redeemable
theology of the cross, and ultimately they seem to conclude that
there isn't.[14]

I read *Proverbs of Ashes* during my second year of seminary for
a feminist theologies class. Not very long before, I had finally confronted my own long-past experiences of sexual violence after years
of avoiding them. The truth overwhelmed me and I was filled with
anger—at the abuser and at God. I struggled with the idea that
God had been with me in that violent experience but had allowed
it to happen. And it made me rage in a new way to then think of a
theology that teaches that God willingly subjected Christ to torture and death and called it grace. Trapped in my own personal
theodicy hell, I was unable to focus on any of my other seminary
courses, but I found liberation in Parker's and Nakashima's words.
I didn't draw the same conclusion that they did about the irre-
deemability of cross theology, but their book gave me permission
to protest my own experience of violence, a God that allowed it to
happen, and a theology that sanctions violence as holy.

Inspired by them, I wrote a series of poems processing my
anger, grief, and doubt. And then I made my protest physical and
public in my final project for that class. I invited close and trusted
friends to my house. We broke bread and drank wine. I let each
friend choose two of the poems I had written and write them with
Sharpie markers on parts of my body that I wanted to reclaim
even as I wanted to reclaim my faith and my God from harmful,
abusive theologies. Like Idit, and Parker and Brock, I looked back
and questioned in defiance—protesting against evil I had experienced. Only then, in equal protest and equally defiant hope,
with friends gathered around me, could I look forward in faith.
Protest, even against God, and even when it cannot change what
is protested against, can be powerful, holy, and healing.

## Protest as Moral Obligation
### (How Protest Can Save Us)

We seem to be, in these days, in a particularly potent season of protests. In 2010, the Arab Spring protests against oppressive governmental regimes ignited revolution in Tunisia, Egypt, Libya, Bahrain, Syria, and Yemen. From September to November in 2011, protesters assembled in Zuccotti Park in New York City under the collective banner "Occupy Wall Street"—protesting social and economic inequality and consumerist culture. In 2013, when George Zimmerman was acquitted in the killing of Trayvon Martin, a hashtag surfaced in response, proclaiming "Black lives matter." A year later, in the wake of the deaths of Mike Brown and Eric Garner, protests in Ferguson, Missouri, catalyzed that hashtag into a nationally recognized movement for racial justice.

In January of 2017, the Women's March assembled somewhere between five hundred thousand and one million people in Washington, DC, and an estimated five million people worldwide, making it the largest single protest in US history. And in March of 2018, a group of high school students who had just survived the shooting at Marjory Stoneman Douglas High School in Florida galvanized tens of thousands of people to "March for Our Lives" in protest against gun violence and to call for stricter gun regulation. Over the last year, the hashtag #MeToo has becoming a rallying call for women and others to speak out against sexual violence. It's been joined by #ChurchToo, started by Emily Joy and Hannah Paasch to call out sexual violence and abuse in churches specifically, with a particular emphasis on evangelical churches.

There are others, of course. We live in times of upheaval, unrest, and discord. People aren't content to sit quietly in the face of inequality, injustice, or even dissatisfaction and silencing. Perhaps even more significantly, they have more opportunities than ever to respond, because we also live in times of unprecedented access to one another and global conversations via social media. While some criticize social media-based movements as being all talk and no work, or "slacktivism," as it is sometimes called, what's also true is that social media, the internet, and diversification of news media have all given microphones to people and communities that have long been silenced. The narrative isn't growing more complex. We're simply, finally, hearing more than one or a select few voices. We're beginning to recognize how complex the narrative has always been and still is.

While many of the aforementioned protests are either entirely or predominantly secular in nature, there are church-based protest movements too. At the organization I work for, Sojourners, in Washington, DC, activists have been protesting and meeting with legislators to lobby for racial justice, immigration reform, justice for women and girls, efforts to stop climate change, eradication of poverty, and nonviolence and peace for nearly half a century. In North Carolina, the Moral Mondays movement started in 2013 is still going strong. The movement was partly founded and is still largely led by Protestant minister William Barber, who at the time was also the head of the North Carolina chapter of the National Association for the Advancement of Colored People. Following in the footsteps of the 1960s civil rights leaders, the Moral Mondays movement focuses on sustained, regular civil disobedience and nonviolent protest—in opposition to policies and legislation that the protesters believe negatively impact both citizens and the environment. The movement has spread and found support in other states, including Alabama, Arkansas, Florida, Georgia, Indiana, Mississippi, New York, Ohio, Pennsylvania, Tennessee, and Wisconsin.

Barber also went on to co-lead, along with the Rev. Dr. Liz Theoharis, the 2018 Poor People's Campaign, a forty-day public anti-poverty protest in the spirit of the 1968 campaign of the same name. In an interview with Duke University's *Faith and Leadership*, Barber speaks about why his faith compels him to engage in protest and activism work. "I think the first thing—and this might seem simplistic—is we have to begin to preach the gospel in our churches. Not merely attempt to quarantine the church from the issues in the world but to have the courage, as Karl Barth once said, to hold the Bible in one hand and the newspaper in the other."[15] He goes on to say, "The issues that I believe Christ would have us be concerned about are the very ones that he lifted up in his first public sermon: the poor, the sick, the imprisoned, the bruised, the broken, the blind, and all of those who have been made to feel unacceptable."

Of course, protest occurs for a lot of different reasons and in service to an endless myriad of causes. Not every protest has genuine justice in mind. It's hard to believe the hateful action of Westboro Baptist seeks to spread anything other than condemnation and hate. Still others have one perspective on justice in mind, while counterprotesters make an opposing claim. Every year, proponents of banning abortion in the name of protecting the unborn stage a March for Life in Washington, DC. Others protest the march in the name of reproductive justice. People may not always agree on what constitutes a just reason for protest, but righteous protest lifts up stories that have been long silenced, ignored, or actively oppressed.

At its best, protest names that which has been forbidden to be named. It amplifies voices speaking truths that society or the powers that be or the status quo would rather drown out. It gives perspectives that might otherwise be erased. It shines a light on injustice, on brokenness, and on evil so that—when they are seen for what they are—the world might be compelled to respond.

So, what does this mean for us? To be a faithful Christian in a broken world is to live in protest of what does the breaking and what is broken, in the name of love, wholeness, and healing. Faith ought to be, by its very nature, an inconvenient disruption to "just the way things are." And if we are the ones being made uncomfortable by a protest, it's worth asking ourselves, "What truth are we afraid to hear?"

# Chapter Nine

# The Gift of Hunger

One of my favorite jokes from the late comedian Mitch Hedberg goes something like this: "You know how when you go to a restaurant on the weekend, and it's crowded so they have a wait list? And when a table's ready, they'll call out 'Dufresne, party of two! . . . Dufresne, party of two!' But then if the Dufresnes never show up, they just move right on to the next name. 'Bush, party of three!' Wait a minute. What happened to the Dufresnes? No one seems to care. How can you people eat at a time like this? Y'all are selfish. PEOPLE ARE MISSING. The Dufresnes are in somebody's trunk right now with duct tape over their mouths. And they're hungry! That's a double whammy. We need some help. 'Bush, search party of three.' You can eat when you find the Dufresnes."

I love this joke because it does what so many great jokes do—it points to something common that we never even spare a moment to think about. What *did* happen to the people who never showed up at the host stand when their name was called? Presumably, they just gave up and left for a restaurant with a shorter wait time—but why has the thought never even crossed my mind? But I also love this joke because it, maybe unintentionally, points to another unrelenting truth: We gotta eat. All of us. No exceptions. And when our name gets called, our hunger sometimes drives us to leave others behind rather than risk going hungry ourselves.

One of the reasons I love the sacrament of Communion is that it takes an ordinary (even desperate, at times) moment of need and makes it an extraordinary invitation to abundance and grace. Communion isn't about a once-in-a-lifetime moment. It's about the everyday. The messy and the necessary. It is grace meeting us in the mundane. Baptism happens once, for most of us, but Communion walks with us our entire lives. It finds us over and over and over again, wherever we are. It's there to meet us when we walk down the aisle only half paying attention—our minds distracted by other worries. It's there to meet us when we show up hungover from partying too hard the night before. It's there to meet us when our parents drag us or guilt us into going. It's there to meet us when we walk forward trembling, tears in our eyes, because it's almost painful to believe we belong.

When I was a kid, Communion felt to me like being known, being part of a community. Those walks down the aisle every month, and later on rarer occasions when I was home from school or visiting on holidays, always felt both like a special treat and like coming home to something—to God. The first time I served Communion, I was in seminary, and it was during our weekly chapel service. I held the chalice next to my worship professor, who offered the bread. I knew everyone who came forward, so as I offered them the cup, I called them by name as I believed God would, saying, "This is the cup of the new covenant, poured out for you." It was one of the holiest experiences of my life, not because I felt important or sacred, but because I didn't. I knew that I, in that moment, was just a vessel, holding the cup in the meeting place between God and each person.

For all the ways that Communion is there for us—it's also not there just for us. It's for everyone. For that church lady who always gives you the stink eye. For your obnoxious little brother. For your sweet older neighbor who lives alone and for the man who sleeps on the bench outside. A seminary professor of mine wrote a poem once about serving Communion as his ex-mother-in-law came forward to receive, and reckoning with the unwieldy expansiveness of God's love and grace that doesn't care one iota about our own divisions. We live in a world that proclaims "survival of the fittest"—take what you can no matter what it does to others, because there isn't enough to go around. Communion tells us "survival for everyone," "enough for everyone," and "more together." At the Table, everyone has a place. I know that many traditions believe that Communion requires some sort of formal profession of faith or provable worthiness, but I don't believe the Table requires anything of us except that we show up hungry. And when we don't show up, it saves a place for us.

Communion is rooted in hunger and thirst—a universal experience. We all need food and drink. We all experience hunger. We all die if our hunger isn't met. And in this way, at the Table, we are all equal. Human. Needy. Vulnerable. Political prestige or worldly wealth cannot keep you alive without food and drink to sustain your body. It's also worth pointing out that the hunger we experience—and which Communion points to—isn't just physical hunger. It's also spiritual hunger. Emotional hunger. We crave belonging, community, sustenance in body and spirit. We wilt and fade and even die in the absence of any of these things. And Communion is God's promise that all that need will be met. Food, drink, faith, and belonging. Not separately, not individually, but together.

### Fear of Scarcity
### (How Hunger Separates Us)

About a year ago, while I was packing up to move out of my apartment, I turned on my TV to have a mindless distraction in the background and quickly got sucked into a television show called *The 100*. The show airs on the CW, a network that targets primarily young people, and so, unsurprisingly, the show itself focuses mostly on a group of one hundred teenagers. At the outset of the series, they live aboard a cobbled-together space station where the remnants of humanity wait for Earth to become habitable again after the fallout from apocalyptic nuclear war ninety-seven years earlier. It's supposed to take two hundred years, and so the humans are left to survive together on bare rations, limited resources, and a draconian legal system in which any adult who breaks any law (and there are many) is executed by being floated out into the vacuum of space. Those under eighteen who commit crimes are relegated to the Skybox to await further evaluation on their eighteenth birthday.

The one hundred teens of the show are the full population of the Skybox, and in the first episode they are sent in a shuttle down to Earth to see if the planet has somehow become habitable 103 years early. Essentially, the space station is failing, and the adults in charge have deemed these delinquent children expendable. If the planet is safe, everyone survives. If it isn't, the absence of one hundred lives gives those remaining on the space station a little more time and resources to figure out how to survive. Thus begins an ongoing and cascading series of horrific decisions that define the series. Over and over again, various characters sacrifice others, kill, steal, and make all manner of ethically dubious or flat-out horrifying moves in the name of survival, of protecting their own. They live an existence of incredible scarcity with limited food, shelter, medical care, and weapons, and—because of these limitations—increasingly limited humanity. Every time one of these characters does something horrific to someone else in the name of helping *their people* survive, they reckon with their guilt and others' horror by saying the same line, "We had no choice."

Thankfully, we do not occupy a postapocalyptic planet—nor one with such limited resources that we're forced to sacrifice our children to preserve our own safety. And yet, one of the most eerie things about this show is how not entirely irrelevant it feels to our current reality in 2019. We may not be postapocalypse, but the news sometimes paints a picture of fear and risk and danger so potent that it seems as if we may indeed be pre-apocalypse, and making all the ethically questionable and other-sacrificing decisions that go along with it.

A phrase that has grown popular in the circles I run in is the "myth of scarcity." The concept behind it is that we are plagued by this phantom of an idea that there is not enough to go around. Not enough power. Not enough wealth. Not enough jobs. Not enough food. Not enough love. The thing is: it's a lie. And the people most likely to believe that there isn't enough to go around are the people who have more than enough. Writing on this myth, Father Richard Rohr quotes Lynne Twist's list of three core beliefs that fuel an economy of scarcity.[1] First, "there's not enough to go around." Second, "more is better." And finally, "that's just the way it is." Together, these three myths compel us to believe that we must cling to what we have, and relentlessly acquire more, or else risk being the one without. Moreover, these myths instill in us a deep conviction that this reality cannot be changed.

Few things erect walls between us more quickly or fiercely than our fear of scarcity. As I write this, hundreds of migrants in a caravan are making their way to the US border, seeking asylum, and igniting conversations in the United States around immigration and what it means to welcome the stranger. Indeed, these conversations have been increasingly prevalent over the past two years, as the current administration has made proclamations about building border walls and others have responded with adamant protest. In these conversations, people bring up safety, legality, and "taking care of our own first." And undergirding these conversations is a very real fear that, if the doors to our country are wide-open for people to pour in, we will not have enough for ourselves.

This fear is why we hunker down in communities of our own kith and kin. It's why the eight richest people in the world share, between them, the same amount of wealth as the poorest 50 percent of the world's population, according to a study by Oxfam in early 2017.[2] Certainly we recognize that others have less than us, even to an extreme degree, but we also tell ourselves that others have more, and we don't have enough to share. We deal with the morality of this dilemma by separating ourselves from the humanity of those who suffer and die for lack of basic necessities like food and water. We say that it's too big a problem for us to solve, or else it isn't our responsibility. We have enough problems and concerns of our own to be getting on with; we can't spare a thought for "those people, over there."

And to be clear, for most of us, most of the time, this isn't a throwaway thought. It's a very real fear. Since my childhood, my dad has struggled financially. He has spent periods of time without secure housing, without the guarantee of food. He's faced medical crises without coverage or support. And I have struggled from my own vantage point of nonprofit salary and job insecurity to know how best to support him. I cannot tell you how many times I have passed a person asking for money and thought to myself, defensively, "If I had anything to spare, I would be helping my father."

I would not dare to suggest that there is a gift to be found in hunger without first clarifying that I do not mean *unmet* hunger. Unmet hunger isn't a gift, it's a crime. Every day in this world and this country, countless people die for lack of food and clean water. Someone once told me that hunger is one of the most devastating issues affecting humanity that is entirely within our capacity to resolve, but we don't. In a world where some have so much that it constantly goes to waste, the fact that others die from lack is nothing more or less than a dereliction of duty and the denial of humanity. And elsewhere, many whose physical needs may be met are still deprived of community, acceptance, belonging—and for them too, often the ultimate result is death. We can and must do better by one another.

I don't presume to know the perfect economic or governmental solution to the global epidemic of hunger. And though I certainly have opinions I could offer, my point here isn't to give a prescription. It is to say that what separates us, when it comes to hunger, is our fearful belief that somebody has to go hungry so that we don't. And in order to deal with that presumption, we make those people who we believe must go hungry somehow "other," different from us. Less worthy. Less beloved.

The promise of the Table—of Communion—is that everyone is worthy and beloved. Everyone. Equally. No exceptions. And no one deserves to go hungry—physically or spiritually. Recently, a ministry colleague, Lura N. Groen, said it this way: "Christians can, and do, and probably should, have political differences about the best policies for making sure everyone has enough to eat. Christians should not be disagreeing that this is a goal."[3]

This deep, inescapable vulnerability that we all share—our hunger for sustenance in body and in spirit—is also our common humanity. And it is where God meets us and claims us and binds us up together.

## Timely Abundance
### (Hunger in the Bible)

It's no secret that Jesus liked a good meal. Many of his key ministry moments occurred around shared table, with perhaps the most famous among them being the feeding of the multitude. There are actually two stories about this in the Bible—a feeding of five thousand, which appears in all four Gospels, and a feeding of four thousand, which appears in Matthew and Mark. In every account, Jesus is speaking before a large, hungry crowd, and he doesn't have enough food to offer them. Somehow, the meager offerings of a few loaves of bread and fish (numbers vary, depending on which miracle you're reading about) become an abundance to not only feed the crowd, but have leftovers besides.

In John's version of the feeding of the five thousand (John 6:1–14), Jesus asks his disciple Philip where they're going to buy food for the crowd, as a test. Philip only tells him that six months' wages wouldn't buy enough bread to feed the thousands gathered. Andrew chimes in that a small boy has five loaves and two fish. Maybe Andrew felt foolish, because he's quick to follow up with the question, "What are they among so many people?" These disciples are living a reality of scarcity, or so it seems. But Jesus has other ideas.

Andrew's doubting question is an excellent setup, it turns out. Jesus commands his followers to have the people sit down, and then he distributes the fish and bread among the crowd. Here's my favorite part, "as much as they want," Jesus says, encouraging everyone to take their fill. I have to believe the disciples were dubious about the confident extravagance of this instruction. And yet, the people do take all that they want, and when everyone has eaten to their satisfaction, the disciples gather up all the broken remnants, *twelve full baskets of food.* These broken remainders add up to more food than they began with.

It's hard to say what exactly happened in this miracle. Did Jesus miraculously amplify the boy's contribution to make more than enough to abundantly feed five thousand people? Or does this gathered multitude, upon encountering the boy's generosity and Jesus' confidence, give of their own limited supply to the point that every person is fully sated and then some? Generally, the latter interpretation seems to belong to cynics and skeptics, unwilling to assign to Christ the full power of his divinity. But I'll admit that I prefer it. The former reading suggests that Jesus himself can create an abundance where there is only scarcity and lack, all on his own. But the latter reading suggests that Jesus inspires that ability in us. Perhaps Jesus was confident not in his own magical superpowers, but in humanity's ability to care for one another in a moment of shared need and vulnerability.

In fact, if my favorite part of this story is Jesus' ridiculous invitation to allow people to take "as much as they want"—suggesting that what we desire when we are not fueled by greed and scarcity is more than enough to satisfy us and meet the needs of others—my second favorite part of this story isn't actually written down at all. Or at least, it's only briefly alluded to. After everyone has eaten, Jesus instructs the disciples to gather the remnants "so that nothing may be lost." The text doesn't tell us what becomes of those leftovers. But I love to imagine that a few folks volunteered to take them somewhere else where food was in short supply. And that maybe, in that new place, other folks were inspired by that generous offering to give what they could, and perhaps that meant that once again, everyone was able to have as much as they wanted, with leftovers to spare. And maybe those leftovers, too, were shared with other folks in need, and on and on so that one great meal has continued with baskets of broken remnants and miracles of unexpected abundance.

This isn't the only significant meal in Jesus' ministry, of course. Nor is it the only time he emphasizes abundance in the face of limitation and brokenness. This is what the Last Supper is all about. Hours before his betrayal and arrest, Jesus gathers in a small, warmly lit room with his closest friends and followers. Judas is there. Judas who, Jesus already knows, has sold him out and will lead him straight into the arms of his murderers. Peter is there too—who loves Jesus so much and who gets it wrong so often and will shortly get it wrong again, three times over. John too, into whose trust Jesus will place his mother's care, and vice versa. They're all there, hungry for food at the end of a long day, lips eager for the taste of wine, hearts hungry for time and more teaching from this man they love and follow, starving for wholeness, choking on their own inescapable brokenness.

And Jesus takes bread, blesses it, breaks it, and gives it to them. And he says, "This bread is my body, broken for you. Take, eat of it, all of you. Do this in remembrance of me." And after the bread is passed he pours the wine, offering them the cup of the new covenant. And here again—not in a field in the midst of thousands, bolstered by his own confidence, but in a cramped, musty upper room with those he loves most, who will soon fail him, and feeling the first tremors of his own fear and doubt—Jesus takes the hunger and brokenness that are present and turns them into a promise of healing, of wholeness, of new life, and of him forever present.

God reaches us not by making us like God—immortal and pure and perfect—but by becoming like us: human, vulnerable, finite. In the same way, Jesus doesn't invite us into grace by some extraordinary, unimaginable, magical means, but by the utter ordinariness of a meal to satisfy the pang in our gut. Perhaps when Jesus said, "Do this in remembrance of me," he imagined the long centuries of churches gathered together in the rite of Eucharist, whether with fancy plates or scattered crumbs on cheap wooden tables, but I deeply believe that he also meant, *"Every day, with that twist of your stomach or the chime of the clock reminding you that it's time to eat, remember me. Remember that you are not alone, that you are not lost, and that you are loved."* Just as Christ's power is made perfect in weakness, so too does grace find us and bind us to Christ and one another not in our strength, but in our vulnerabilities. In our human need. In that which we would perish without.

On the road to Emmaus, Jesus makes this point again (Luke 24:13–35). Cleopas and the unnamed disciple are walking along, heavy with their own grief, and they do not recognize Jesus when they come upon him. It's no wonder really; he's been dead. They aren't exactly expecting to encounter him. But when he sits to eat with them and breaks bread, their eyes are suddenly opened and they recognize him. Again, Jesus reaches them not in his divinity or perfection, but in the simple, ordinary human realities of hunger and brokenness.

I love every single one of these stories. I love that Jesus makes food and shared table the crux (pun intended) of his ministry. But my favorite meal story about Jesus isn't one of these famous ones. It's not one we talk about very much at all. Or, more accurately, it's not a story where we often focus on the meal. It's John's account of a woman anointing Jesus' feet with perfume, and in John's story, the woman is Mary and the encounter happens at a dinner party at Lazarus's house at Bethany (John 12:1–11). When this story comes up in the Revised Common Lectionary— that is, the weekly selection of Scriptures that provide rhythm to our year and which many pastors preach from—the designated passage stops just short of the three verses that provide context for this dinner. The most remarkable thing about the story isn't Mary's decision to spill costly perfume in Jesus' honor. Don't get me wrong—that *is* a remarkable moment. But the three short verses after the scene reveal that, even as Jesus and his followers sit at table together arguing about perfume, the chief priests are plotting to kill Lazarus because of his role in leading people to Jesus. Shortly after this, the heavy events of Jesus' final days will unfold, and Jesus already knows it's coming.

Given all this background information, I have to admit that my first instinct is to wonder, as Mitch Hedberg did, "What the *hell* are they doing eating at a time like this?" Why are they wasting time arguing about perfume and sitting around drinking wine and passing hors d'oeuvres when there are corrupt power players plotting assassinations a few miles away? Somewhere in the midst of this emphatic reaction to this story, I remember that Jesus rarely does things by accident. And so I wonder again, "What *is* he doing, going to a dinner party at a time like this?"

I think he's making a point, and the others with him. The atmosphere is growing heavy, darkness is looming, truly devastating calamity is already on its way. And here is the Son of God, making time to sit at table with his friends and loved ones. He is saying, "This is *precisely* the time to eat." Shared table, for Jesus, is a ministry of fellowship. It is a joining together in the midst of vulnerability and need for both food and connection. And in this ill-timed, or maybe powerfully timed, dinner party, with its moral lessons about the gift of extravagant presence, Jesus says to us that when the bitter and broken forces of this world are bearing down, the most powerful thing we can do is acknowledge our hunger, our need, and choose to be present to one another.

In the feeding of the multitude, Jesus shows us that the power to find abundance in our shared brokenness and limited offerings is already in our midst. In the Last Supper, Jesus shows us that when we come hungry to the table and one another, we find healing and wholeness. On the road to Emmaus, he is made known to us in the ordinary humanness of rumbling stomachs and eyes hungry with grief. And at Bethany, Jesus tells us that the hunger that twists our stomachs daily, that reminds and compels us to seek out a table and friend or family member or even a stranger with whom to sit and eat—that hunger can hold back the tide of evil, even if only for a time.

Of course, Jesus isn't the first indication that God offers grace through sustenance. All those centuries before God took on flesh in the body of a Jewish infant, or tore unleavened bread with his own dusty hands, God was providing manna to the Israelites lost in the wilderness of this world. They couldn't hold onto it. But daily, as their hunger drove them to seek out hope, they found it anew, and they were fed, and they went on. Together.

## Cravings, Community, and Connection
### (How Hunger Can Save Us)

It's fair to say that my relationship with food and hunger is complicated. It hasn't always been that way. I grew up in the heart of the South, lucky enough to eat homemade meals cooked by Mom nearly every night of the week. We were a "meat and two" kind of family, as they say—a lot of hearty meals: meatloaf and porkchops and fried chicken with mashed potatoes, mac and cheese, green beans, and lima beans, and always some buttered biscuits. Food has, for most of my life, been a comfort. It has served as nostalgia and memory of people and places that have mattered to me, as a type of homecoming, as an anchor, and as a way of sharing who I am with other people I love and care about.

However, over time, food and disordered eating have also become a part of how I manifest my anxiety. When I am really anxious, I cannot eat—I'm too nauseous. And when I'm depressed, I cannot bring myself to care enough to eat. A few years ago, I went through a time of both depression and anxiety so bad that I lost a dangerous amount of weight in a fairly short period of time. I moved past the point of people still giving me compliments on my weight loss even after it was no longer healthy, to people flat-out asking me if I was sick. And I was. Some days, I couldn't stomach anything, and I subsisted entirely on Diet Coke. In that season, and in other times like it, I haven't felt hungry at all.

I know that hunger is a complicated issue. It's complicated because so many people in this world right now are going hungry and we aren't doing enough to stop that from happening. It's complicated because so many other people are struggling with disordered eating that can look a million different ways—both noticeable and not. And we, as a culture, have a terrible practice of talking about food and health in incredibly harmful ways. All of that is true.

For me, the hunger I've felt my whole life at the thought of a good home-cooked meal or my favorite dish has taken on deeper meaning since my struggles with eating. Now, when I feel hungry and am then able to satisfy that hunger with food, it feels like a gift. I am human, and I am imperfect, and I am fragile, but I am also here. Hungry for sustenance and life.

When I say hunger has a gift to offer, I mean the way that Jesus used hunger—as a basic, universal human experience—to draw us together. Our hunger for food reminds us of our connection to the rest of creation. We cannot exist entirely in isolation. We need the fruit of the earth, and we need the hands that harvest it—which often aren't our own. Communion—as a symbol of

God's deep love meeting our deep hunger—is a holy moment between our Creator and us. But I also love to remember that it is a moment that connects us to so much else. Yes, the hands that offer us the bread and hold out the cup, but also the hands that shaped clay or metal or glass or porcelain into plate and chalice. The hands that rolled the dough, the hands that picked the grains, and the hands that tended the seeds that grew into those grains. And of course, it connects us to the earthy elements that became the clay or metal that became the plate and cup, and to the grapes that became the wine and juice, to the seeds that became the wheat and dough, and even, I'd say, to all the others—human and animal—who eat of that same earth as well. It isn't just Communion that points to this connection. It's every meal. It's every time we meet our hunger with table and find comfort there.

I've mentioned throughout this chapter that we experience more than one type of hunger, which I've mostly referred to as physical and spiritual. By physical hunger, I mean, naturally, our need for food and drink. By spiritual hunger, I don't necessarily mean a hunger for God or faith—although I do think many of us hunger for those things. I think on a more universal level, though, we are all craving some sense of belonging to something bigger than ourselves. Whether that's a divine being, or the universe, or a family or community—even the most introverted among us seem to have a natural need for company and connection. It's true that a shared meal can be a powerful vehicle for that, but it's not the only way we satisfy that particular intangible hunger.

We make friends and neighbors. We dive headfirst into best friendships and never look back. We have siblinghoods, of blood and other bonds. We develop relationships and groups and crews and communities around shared interests and values. We do this often most powerfully when those commonalities are up against a world of opposition. The groups of LGBTQ Christian leaders that I have been a part of have developed especially strong bonds because of the ways in which it has felt as if the whole world was against us, finding strength in our care for one another. Sometimes these bonds are formed around the most important things: a shared belief, a shared passion, a shared hardship, or a common commitment to a particular justice issue. Sometimes, the binding agent can be much more mundane, and yet still somehow holy and powerful.

I grew up the youngest of four in a blended family, and the exact middle child of nine grandchildren on my stepdad's side of the family. I didn't have any cousins on my mom's side, and didn't know my cousins on my dad's side very well growing up, so I was thrilled to be absorbed into a giant, boisterous southern family. It was a fun community to grow up in, filled with stories and games and arguments and, yes, good food. My grandparents and aunts and uncles did a great job of making my brother and me feel loved and accepted. Still, because life is life, I always felt a little set apart. After all, no matter how loved we were, we were also . . . different. My grandparents had a wall in their house displaying baby photos of all the grandchildren, except my brother and me. It makes sense, I guess—they weren't around when we were babies. And of course, on occasion, as we all sat together on holidays, there'd be stories about the time "before." Before my stepdad married my mom, and thus before *us*. I'm not sure how much my brother noticed or cared, but because I was very much sensitive to feeling left out, it stuck somewhere in the back of my mind all my years of growing up.

And then I turned eighteen, and I went to college at the University of Georgia. If you know anything about the South, you've probably heard someone, somewhere, say that in the South, college football isn't just a pastime, it's a religion. I can attest to that. I grew up going to tailgates on Saturdays in the fall with my extended family. We were an Auburn family—nearly everyone had gone there for generations. I went to Georgia and had to put my Auburn love on a shelf, but I took my love of college football with me. The autumn of my freshman year, my grandparents threw a big fiftieth wedding anniversary shindig at a country club in Auburn, where they were living. I pouted about coming to it, because it meant giving up my ticket to watch Georgia play LSU—the school I'd almost attended.

That was a big football weekend all around. Not only was Georgia playing LSU, but Auburn was playing Tennessee, which had just beaten Georgia the week before. And South Carolina—the team my brother and his future wife rooted for—was playing Auburn's biggest rival, making them our one universal enemy.

We all gathered for my grandparents' party, laughing and getting away with a few alcoholic drinks a couple years too early. And every once in a while, a couple of people would disappear down the hallway to check the game scores in the bar of the country club. The rest of us kept our grandparents occupied so they wouldn't question the absences and then be hurt to learn we were all thinking about the football games.

The time came to eat, and we sat down at three large tables, all facing each other. My grandfather got up to welcome everyone. He said, "I'd like to say a few words, but before I do—I think there's something that needs to be said." I remember bracing myself for what I was sure would be a scathing word about our distracted football fandom. To my surprise, he pulled out a slip of paper and read off the latest scores of all three games, which he, too, had been keeping tabs on all evening, as it turned out.

All three of our teams won their games that night, and we returned from the party to our hotel, which sat just across the street from Toomer's Corner, where the campus of Auburn University meets the small downtown. By tradition at Auburn, when the football team wins a game, students rush to Toomer's Corner and roll its giant old oak trees with toilet paper.

That night, as I reached the hotel lobby, trailing behind my parents and aunts and uncles, they passed me, running back out the front doors. "Where are you going?!" I called to them, confused. "Toomer's Corner! Come on!" they shouted back. It was only then that I noticed the rolls of toilet paper tucked under their arms. My mom nodded in the direction of the lobby bathroom. I was flustered but eager to follow, so I grabbed a roll and ran to join them. That night ended with my entire family—grandparents, parents, aunts and uncles, cousins, siblings, and me—standing amid several hundred young Auburn students, throwing rolls of toilet paper around ancient oak branches and laughing into the night. As long as I live, I will never forget the feeling of that moment—because in that moment, standing there among my family, I knew with absolute certainty that I belonged.

Football is not a religion, even if sometimes it feels like it. Not really. It's not even an unquestionable sport, if I'm being honest, given all the concerns about head injuries and exploitation. And toilet-papering trees is a foolhardy activity. But I can also tell you this: on that night, football and its ridiculous traditions were the bread and cup that satisfied a young girl's lifelong hunger to know that she belonged in her own family. Good luck trying to convince me there isn't something holy in that.

Our hunger—when we do not let our fear of scarcity drive us apart—draws us together. It reminds us that we need one another and that we need to care for one another. It reminds us that we need to be a part of something bigger than ourselves, and that we are. It reminds us that that need is our strength, because even on the worst days, when it seems so certain that brokenness and division and hate will win—we still wake up hungry. And that hunger reminds us that we need something different—that we need each other. And it will not let us be satisfied with anything less.

## Hunger as Holy Home: A Case Study

When it comes to imagining the implications of this for us as human beings, as people of faith, the best way I can think to explain it is one more story. It is the story of a church that allowed itself to become the answer to someone's hunger in a way that it never could have imagined, simply because it showed up with an open table, again and again.

For many years, on the wide thoroughfare of Broad Street in Center City Philadelphia, there sat a great church called Chambers-Wylie Memorial Presbyterian. Many of Philadelphia's social elite came there on Sunday mornings, dressed in their best attire, to greet one another, feel at home, and worship God. Over time, though, the neighborhood changed, those social elites moved out to the suburbs, the congregation dwindled, and the building fell into disrepair. By the early 2000s, Chambers-Wylie Memorial Presbyterian was all but dead, its building hardly more than a hollowed-out shell.

And then one day some young seminarians and ministers came upon the old building, and they imagined new life and new community springing up within. They began a new church, intended for the many young artists who frequented that part of town. But that wasn't who came—or it wasn't the only people who came. There were artists, yes, but there were also people who lived and slept in Center City, people who were facing job insecurity, food insecurity, housing insecurity or homelessness, and mental health struggles. These people began to come too. And so the founders of this church, which came to be known as Broad Street Ministry, realized that their church needed to offer more than cool arts opportunities for its people. It began to offer social services, access to medical care and art therapy and clothing, mailing addresses, and it began to serve meals several times a week.

Recognizing that for many members of their community, poverty and homelessness were traumatic experiences in and of themselves, Broad Street sought to offer a trauma-informed ministry. It ripped the old pews out of its sanctuary and began serving its meals in the stained-glass room at round tables, serving everyone at the table at the same time. They made sure that everyone got what they needed and that no one had to stand in line and fear that there might not be enough. They hired a chef to provide healthy, gourmet, restaurant-quality meals that honored the bodies and the dignity of those who ate them. Their community grew.

Years ago, when I was in the middle of seminary, I spent one summer in Philly working for Broad Street Ministry as my field education internship. My work was primarily with their alternative youth mission program, so I spent less time with their meal program, which they called Breaking Bread. Every Wednesday morning, we gathered as a staff to debrief the week before and make plans for the week ahead. One Wednesday morning, one of my coworkers—the head of our social services program—told the staff that at the previous evening's meal, one particular guest sat down at a table to eat.

It was such a simple story. It seemed like an odd thing to make a point of sharing. Except that this particular guest had been coming to Broad Street for meals for years. He had been traumatized, like so many others, by his experiences on the streets. And in all those years that he had been coming to Broad Street, he had eaten every single meal standing up, with his back against the wall. It was a protective move, you see.

But on this otherwise ordinary Tuesday, this man—this child of God—had sat down at a table, to eat with friends, because he finally felt safe enough and at home enough to do so.

This is a story about hunger. It's a story about a community that showed up in the face of hunger again and again and again, offering a meal and community and solidarity and another, less fearful, story. It's about the hunger for justice we should feel when we are reminded that our siblings are living out these traumatic experiences because of a myth that there is not enough for them. The myth of scarcity, which we make real by believing in it, can only be destroyed once we refuse to be satisfied by anything less than a world where all are welcome and fed and made whole, just like the Table to which Christ invites us. The world tells a story about the fear that hunger can cause in us, but the Table tells us a story about the hope that hunger can drive us toward and the world that waits for us when our hunger for love and belonging and better finally speaks louder than our fear.

# Chapter Ten

# The Gift of Limitations

When I was little, I had big dreams and an even bigger imagination. I tended to believe that nothing was impossible if I wanted it badly enough, and even after life had begun to teach me that this was not, in fact, true, I stubbornly held onto all sorts of impossible beliefs tucked somewhere in the back of my heart. When I think about limitations now, and both the challenges they present and the gifts they offer, two particular stories from my childhood stand out.

The first is the year I accidentally became a donkey. Every year at the church where I grew up, we had a live nativity scene, and church people—adults and children—would take their turns dressing up as the characters associated with Jesus' birth and standing outside beside the main road our church sat on. Passersby could stop and get some hot cocoa and take a closer look. A baby doll stood in for Jesus, and the adults got to play the parts of the three kings and Mary and Joseph, while the older kids donned delicate white robes and golden halos to play the part of angels. The littlest players were left to dress up as shepherds. Over the years, that church has seriously fancied up its nativity game, and now they bring in live sheep and goats and hens and even a very furry Scottish Highland cow. But when I was young, we settled for woolen blankets draped over chairs with cardboard cutouts of animal heads stapled on.

I loved being a part of the live nativity, and I didn't mind being a shepherd, but I *dreamed* of being an angel. The older kids looked so beautiful and magical with their wings and halos, standing on chairs to give the effect of hovering, the outdoor spotlights shining down on them. I bided my time, but internally I was desperate for the day my chance to be an angel would come. And finally, that long-awaited year arrived. With awe, I donned my white robe and halo on that December night and stepped out into . . . a blistering cold. I don't know what the actual temperature was that Georgia evening—and having since spent several winters up North, I imagine it would have been practically balmy for some of you—but I distinctly remember how quickly my fingers and toes began to hurt in the freezing air. The white robes were thin, flimsy things that did nothing to hold in body heat. I remember standing on my plastic chair in the barn, shivering, but determined to hold out. It was finally my year to be an angel, and I told myself, "Angels don't get cold."

Some adult eventually noticed that I was practically turning blue and took pity on me. I was forced to admit that I couldn't last any longer. They took me back inside, and I quickly bundled up in all my regular clothes, but I was devastated at the thought of missing the rest of the live nativity. And so we went back out, and I got down on all fours and draped myself in the heavy gray wool blanket that was standing in for a donkey, placing the cardboard cutout over my face. I was deliciously warm, and throughout the evening the others would pretend to pet me and I would pretend to bray and a stamp a little. And that is the story of how—thanks to bad timing and my utter intolerance for cold—my dreams of being an angel were dashed, and I, instead, became my church's first live animal at the live nativity.

I had a real thing for flying and magic as a kid; in addition to my dreams of angelhood, I was obsessed with Peter Pan. We had an old tape of the stage production, with Mary Martin starring as Peter. I would watch her swing back and forth across the screen, and even though I could tell it wasn't real—she was clearly attached to wires—it still looked magical. I longed to be able to fly through the air like that and visit far-off magical lands and be spunky and unapologetic like Peter was. In fact, my most common recurring dream as a kid was of flying. And it was never easy, like magic. In the dream, I'd stand up in my bed, and it would take all my thinking and believing effort to get airborne and stay that way. For Halloween I went as Peter Pan three years straight, and again a few times as an adult. I knew that flying wasn't really possible outside of dreams. But, I suppose because my first experience of Peter Pan was the stage production, I never even questioned whether I could be Peter Pan as a woman.

There is a children's book called *Amazing Grace* that I learned about from *Reading Rainbow* as a little kid, and because it was in some way about Peter Pan, I loved it.[1] It tells the story of a young black girl named Grace who loves to dress up in costume and act out stories. When her class at school puts on the play version of Peter Pan, she is determined to win the leading role. But other kids in her class tell her that she can't be Peter Pan because she's a girl and Peter Pan is a boy. Or else they tell her that she can't be Peter Pan because she's black, and he's white. Grace gets discouraged, but after a pep talk from her grandmother, she perks up and auditions. Of course, she totally wows everyone, gets cast, and becomes the best Peter Pan her school has ever seen.

Both of these stories exemplify how limitations come into play in our lives. One kind of limitation is what we're capable of and what we can withstand. I really cannot fly, and I really cannot withstand supercold temperatures. We run into limits in our abilities, whether physical, mental, or emotional, and we're forced to accept them and work around them. Certainly we can push ourselves and stretch ourselves and sometimes exceed previous limits. But at other times, we have to think of new strategies, solutions, paths, and futures with our limitations in mind.

Another kind of limitation occurs when society tells us what we cannot do because of who we are or what we look like or where we come from or any number of other factors. Sometimes society has the power to impose those limitations on us, and at other times we can fight against them. But the key in those circumstances is that, in the end, the limitation isn't in our abilities. It's a limitation on other people's part—society's part—a limitation in what they can imagine and understand. Sometimes, we too are guilty of this. Sometimes we're the ones imposing our own limitations of understanding on others.

### Boundaries, Bubbles, and Bias
#### (How Limitations Separate Us)

My inability to bear the cold that night in a temporary stable in suburban Atlanta exposed me to a limit within myself. I could not show up in the way I was expected to show up, given the circumstances around me. That could have meant the end of my participation in the live nativity. In my case, some creative thinking on my part and the part of my community helped me show up in a different way and still be included. But often a difference in ability is all it takes to draw lines in the sand between who is in and who is out. We cannot all do the same things. We are not all skilled in the same ways, nor do we share the same abilities. We don't all speak the same language, have the same financial means or access, or experience the same liberties.

These limitations, whether internal or externally imposed, necessarily create differences between us, and at times even barriers to be overcome, but they don't have to create division. And yet, as I mentioned in the chapter on difference, we exist in a world that privileges certain abilities, characteristics, and qualities—either implicitly or explicitly. We shape our institutions, our policies, our laws, and our society around the limitations and capacities of those who fall within these privileged groups. Everyone else is left to either adapt or, if they can't, be separate and excluded. Though some of us face more challenges in this regard than others, it's likely that everyone has, at some point and even multiple points, been separated out or excluded on the basis of a limitation they experience.

That's not the only way that limitations separate us. To be human is to be limited. The irony is that this is one of the only universals we all share. We are finite, contained, and mortal. We only live one life. We can only exist in one place at a time, and only interact with so many people, do so many different things, visit so many places. Some of us are more limited in these things than others, but not one of us is without limits. We are shaped by our experiences, our contexts, and our abilities. The amalgamation of these things gives each of us our worldview and our particular understanding of truth, of life, and of one another. We are also shaped by our limits—by the experiences and abilities we don't have and the contexts we don't know. These limitations form the borders of our perspective. Because our perspective generally shares the same limits of experience and context that we do, we don't always notice its limits. To us, the truth as we encounter it is just *the truth*. Except it's not. Not really. It's limited. It has borders, barriers, and boundaries. And perhaps even more important, it has a bias. We have a bias.

Biases occur naturally. We tend to gravitate toward what we know, what we understand, and what's familiar. We cling to and elevate what's comfortable. We fight for what we believe to be the truth—even if that truth is actually bounded on all sides by our limited perspective. Inasmuch as biases are naturally occurring, I don't believe they're inherently evil or even inherently bad. Of course I think my nieces and nephews are the cutest kids on the planet, and I defy anyone to convince me otherwise. To me, it even feels like fact. But it's not. I'm just biased because I love them and because I am not as close to any other children as I am to them.

Bias becomes a problem when we don't see it—or when we refuse to acknowledge it for what it is: a limitation. When a bias is accepted as objective fact, it's given undue power. Rather than being recognized as a reflection of the limitations of the bias-holder, it can become a weapon wielded to impose limitations on others. Our bias tells us to give preferential treatment to certain people, certain possibilities. It's not a rational or objective evaluation—or a just one, for that matter—but rather a product of our limited perspective. Of course, bias can lead to prejudice, discrimination, and bigotry, but bias is at work in many cases that are less extreme than that.

There's plenty of talk of bias in the world today, and especially in American politics and media. These days, twenty-four-hour cable news networks provide a constant feed of not just news but also political commentary. People are quick to defend the networks they turn to while lambasting others as mere tools for political manipulation. This accusation has almost certainly been leveled at Fox News more than any other. In fact, in 2004, Robert Greenwald made a documentary called *Outfoxed: Rupert Murdoch's War on Journalism*, which sought to expose the extensive right-wing bias in Fox News's reporting. Greenwald wanted to juxtapose this clear bias with Fox News's tagline of "Fair and Balanced." Of course, Fox News's counterargument has always been that other mainstream media sources are biased in the opposite direction—and they are providing a "fair balance" to those other sources. Members of my family who are devoted Fox viewers make the same argument, and during his presidency, Donald Trump has been both quick and consistent in accusing media outlets other than Fox of being "fake news."

I won't entertain that last claim, but as far as whether other mainstream news sources have a bias? Yes, absolutely they do. It's less a matter of the existence of bias than a matter of degree and open acknowledgment of one's bias. One need only turn on one of MSNBC's many shows to see that it swings in the opposite direction from Fox. Commentators headlining their own shows on these networks aren't reporters—or at least, not exclusively so—they're pundits offering commentary and context to the news they present. Not only do they have a bias, it's part of their work.

I hear lots of people lamenting the bygone days of "good, old-fashioned journalism," when one could count on unbiased reporting and an objective, factual presentation of the truth. On the one hand, I get it. Increasingly I don't know where to look for national or global news that I can trust is presenting only information and not a spin on how I should feel about that information. I seek out local sources and firsthand accounts whenever possible and interpret whatever I read through the lens of potential bias. But it is exhausting and a little overwhelming to think that I don't know of a source I completely trust to tell the truth.

On the other hand, as I often tell people when they make such laments, journalism in those good old days was biased too.

Journalism has always been biased because it's run by humans with their own biases and their own agendas, whether they recognize it or not. What has changed in journalism is, I think, less the development of bias than the diversification of bias. In the past, bias was less evident because journalism on the whole and society collectively were prioritizing the same certain voices telling certain stories in a certain way. Journalism, like many industries, was overwhelmingly controlled by white men, and regardless of their own commitment to objective reporting, this lack of diverse voices automatically affected (and biased) the news presented.

With the rise of the internet and social-media technology, and global access to public platforms for sharing ideas and stories, a universe of voices has arisen, presenting a multitude of narratives to challenge the one that has dominated our societal understanding. As journalism—both formal and informal—has diversified, a market has grown for news and commentary that speaks to different populations and, yes, that aligns with different biases.

As someone who works in advocacy journalism, I don't believe that bias is necessarily bad. *Sojourners* is a magazine and website whose reporting is guided by the values and justice issues we advocate for. In order to know what our bias is, one only needs to go to the "Who We Are" and "What We Cover" pages on our website, and read about our advocacy campaigns: climate change, women and girls, racial justice, poverty, immigration, and peace and nonviolence. These issues—and our particular stance in regard to them—impact the stories we choose to tell and the way we tell them. Within our scope, we seek to present diverse voices and perspectives, but we trust that others are doing the work that doesn't fall within our purview. Our challenge is to be aware of the more subtle, unintentional biases that impact our work—and do what we can to counteract them.

Bias becomes a problem in journalism when it isn't recognized for what it is or presented transparently, or when the reporting being done serves its bias and agenda at the expense of its integrity, choosing intentional dishonesty or manipulation. We consume biased news because we ourselves are biased. And bias in people also becomes a problem when we don't acknowledge it or recognize it for what it is: a product of our limitations, in knowledge, in experience, and in understanding. Our bias becomes a problem when we remain comfortable within its confines and never seek to expand or see what lies beyond our particular perspective.

People tend to gravitate toward sources and arguments that affirm what they already believe. This is a phenomenon called "confirmation bias," and it means that we easily hold onto information that supports our views, while anything that counters our existing belief is more easily dismissed or forgotten and much harder to integrate into our understanding. This doesn't apply only to the news we encounter—it's at work in every facet of our lives, in how we interact and how we interpret our own stories and the world around us. In college, a friend of mine who generally understood herself as someone who was lucky in love experienced a painful rejection. She confided in me that it was painful partly because it seemed to be outside her norm. And yet, she realized, she had experienced rejection before, more than once. But because her desired belief—her narrative bias—was one of romantic success, she tended to remember those experiences while forgetting the rejections. I shared that, for me, as someone constantly struggling with self-doubt, it was the opposite—I tended to remember the rejections and forget the successes. Our biases aren't always positive, but whether they are or are not, they are never the full story.

Confirmation bias is just one part of a larger truth: like clings to like. We are inclined to build community with those who share our values, and more specifically with those who are relatively similar to us in experience, context, and ability. If we do have loved ones with whom we vehemently disagree, we tend to avoid our controversial differences in favor of the things we share. Why? I suspect that it is in part because it takes less work, it's more comfortable. Within that, though, I believe it's also because when we exist within a bubble of relative shared perspective, bias, experience—we don't have to run up against anyone else's limits, or our own limits. Within our own bubbles, we can imagine that our beliefs, knowledge, and experience are sufficient for understanding the world, and in fact our bubble can become our whole world. We may acknowledge on some level that there is more beyond us—other people, other stories, other bubbles—but safely ensconced we don't really have to reckon with that fact as a limit in our own selves.

It is tempting to avoid interrogating our own biases. It's daunting to think of genuinely challenging the limits of our own understanding. But the more we surround ourselves exclusively with that which confirms and matches our own beliefs, the more deeply entrenched our biases become, the less aware of them as bias rather than fact we become, and the permeable boundary of our bubble becomes calcified and hardened into a border wall—with everything beyond it perceived as a threat.

Reckoning with our own limitations means confronting a scary and dangerous truth: that there is more beyond us, beyond our bubbles, our biases, and our personal boundaries. That other people are capable in ways we are not, that they know and understand this world, truth, and God in ways that we simply are not able. Our capacity alone is insufficient. We *need* other people. And the ones we need the most are the ones farthest from us and our comfort zone.

## How God Makes Limitation Sacred
### (Limitations in the Bible)

It's funny that so much of our awe and wonder and worship of God is rooted in God's boundlessness, God's limitlessness, because, frankly, I think God is a little obsessed with limitation. In seminary, I was taught to think of God's entry into human life in the person of Jesus Christ as a sacrifice, a selfless taking-on of the shackles of frailty, finitude, and flesh. I suppose that it would be a pretty profound adjustment for one used to being the all-powerful and infinite Creator of the cosmos. But over and over again we see God choosing people who are inhibited by their own limitations—and not just the standard universal limits of humanity—to do incredible things in this world in God's name. There was Moses, who struggled with public speaking, and Joseph, who was sold into slavery and later jailed. There was David, first a young farm boy and later an easily tempted man. There were the disciples, with all their doubt and failure to get any of the points Jesus was making, and Paul, with his own biases and bigotry to overcome. God seems to not only accept limitations but also delight in them—in the unexpected things born from them, and in the creative ways that they can be overcome.

Let's talk about Samuel and Eli. I love this story, in part precisely because of the point it makes about limitations: sometimes, two people's limitations can complement each other in such a way that together they are able to accomplish what neither could do alone. Samuel is the son of Hannah, who spent years crying to God about her infertility and promised that, should she conceive, she would dedicate the child's life to God. Indeed she did, and Samuel grew up in the temple and went on to be a mighty prophet, overseeing Israel's transition from judges to kings, warranting a full two books in the Bible with his name stamped on. But when God first calls Samuel, he's just a boy. He doesn't have the experience yet to recognize God's voice, or, as the Scriptures tell us, "the word of the LORD had not yet been revealed to him" (1 Sam. 3:7). In short, Samuel is limited by his youth and inexperience.

Meanwhile, Samuel is living at the temple and studying under the priest Eli, who has grown old and frail and is losing his eyesight. Eli is limited by his old age, by his own shortcomings as a priest, by his failing senses and his growing frailty. It falls to Samuel to stay in the temple with the lamp of God, which has not yet gone out, while Eli lies down in bed. When Samuel hears a voice calling his name, he believes, in his youthful innocence, that it's Eli calling out to him. Ever eager to please, Samuel goes to Eli straightaway, only to discover that Eli has not called him at all. At the priest's instruction, Samuel returns to the temple, and twice more the voice calls to him and twice more he returns to Eli. Finally, it is Eli—in his hard-earned wisdom—who realizes what's really going on: God is at work. And so he tells Samuel to return once more and when next he hears the voice, to say, "Speak, LORD, for your servant is listening" (3:9). Samuel heeds Eli's instruction and is called upon by God, and so his journey as great prophet begins. God uses Samuel to lead the people in a way that Eli, with the limitations of his age, no longer can. But on his own, Samuel cannot recognize God's call because of the limitations of his youth. Eli's wisdom opens the door that Samuel cannot, and Samuel's youth allows him to step through and answer the call that Eli cannot. God uses them both to accomplish the work, relying on the ways each one's abilities and understanding pick up where the other's limitations leave off. Their limits bind them together in the work of God.

In the New Testament, God again relies on the complementary qualities of various people to enable them to pick up where one another's limits leave off, to spread the gospel and grow the church. One of my favorite instances is the story of Lydia and the church in Macedonia. As the story in Acts 16 goes, one night Paul has a dream in which a Macedonian man pleads with him to come and help the people there. And so Paul and his fellow Jesus-followers go to Macedonia, and Paul seeks out the man from his dream. Instead he encounters a woman, Lydia, who is a seller of fine cloth and a God-worshiper. The text tells us that God opens Lydia's heart to everything Paul is saying, and in response Lydia opens up her home to Paul and his crew, and has her entire household baptized. Lydia's home becomes the beginning of the church in Macedonia, and she is often credited with being the first European convert. Lydia needs Paul's teachings to move forward in faith, but Paul needs her too. She keeps the church going and growing, presumably even after Paul has moved on.

This is yet another story of two people whose abilities and access come together to overcome their individual limits and do together what they cannot do alone. But this story makes another point about limitations and God that shouldn't be overlooked. Paul's dream showed him a man. That makes sense. Though women had been a part of Jesus' ministry from the beginning, Paul's context and experience would have taught him to naturally imagine male leadership. Lydia is unexpected. She is an independent businesswoman and a Gentile follower of God from a distant land. Her authority to invite men back to her house likely meant that she was widowed or unmarried. She would have been an unconventional choice for church leader even if Paul hadn't dreamed of a man. Essentially, Lydia and her calling lie beyond the limits of Paul's imagination. And yet, God uses her. And Paul, despite his limits of experience and imagination, trusts God enough to also trust Lydia. Paul accepts that God is at work beyond the limits of his own understanding. And Lydia, for her part, trusts that God is calling her despite the limits imposed on her by virtue of society and her gender, nationality, and marital status. These two, as Eli and Samuel did before them, learn that they are limited, but that God is not. And in that meeting place of human limits and a limitless God, something new and previously unimaginable is born.

There is a concept in theology called the scandal of particularity. It deals with the theological repercussions of believing in a messiah who entered this world as a particular human being—a Jew of Nazareth, a male, a first-century person, a carpenter's son, and a tiny, diaper-wearing baby born in the midst of threat and fear and homelessness. There is something scandalous in the fact that God comes to us in such a particular and limited way. And the scandal—and promise—is this: that by incarnating as a single, unique, particular person, God claims particularity itself as holy, and proclaims that in each of the finest nuances of our particularities God claims us and is also present and at work. To be limited and belong to a limitless God is to be a living testament to and active participant in the creativity of God's Spirit. Of course that is a gift. And it's a gift that all of us have, but not one of us in exactly the same way. When we open ourselves to one another, trade in our bubbles and borders for welcome and connection and learning, God is at work. Amazing things are born at the meeting places of our various limitations. In these intersections, God is at work in ways that we can scarcely imagine.

## It's Not You, It's Us
### (How Limitations Can Save Us)

A few months ago, I preached a sermon for Pride Sunday about Eli and Samuel that had the same title as this chapter, "The Gift of Limitations." After I preached, I posted the sermon on my website and shared the link on my Facebook page. Later that night, I was talking to my dad on the phone and he mentioned that he'd seen the link to my sermon on his news feed, though I don't think he'd read it yet. "How can limitations be a gift?" He asked me, kind of laughing. "I mean, I don't really see how that could be."

As I struggled to explain how our limits mean that we are not enough on our own and that we need something outside ourselves, my dad laughed incredulously and said, "Sweetheart, that doesn't sound like a gift."

Okay. I take his point. In our achievement-oriented, highly individualistic, competitive, and perfectionist society, the idea that we are limited, that we are not enough on our own, that no matter what we do we will still not know or understand or be able to do everything, that we need something and someone beyond ourselves, doesn't exactly sound like a positive. But imagine if what you are able to do and know and understand right now was all there was. Imagine if there was *nothing* beyond that. I don't find any comfort in that idea.

Recognizing just how limited we each are also allows us a glimpse of what it means to believe in a limitless God. We are limited, but God is not—and that means that there is always more to know and learn and understand about God and God's creation. It means that the limits of what we can imagine to be possible are not the actual limits of what is possible—not for God. And because we all have different limits, contexts, experiences, and understandings—we have the power to help each other expand beyond our own limits. We can do and know and believe more together than we can separately. In "The Gift of Difference" (chap. 1), I talked about how, if God is boundless and beyond our comprehension, and we are each different, then we each see a slightly different sliver of who God is. These are our limits, and we need each other to grow in our understanding beyond those limits.

The gift of our limitations is that they give us humility. And that may not sound like the best gift, but it is an invitation to draw closer to one another, to trust in and need one another, to challenge the limits. We should be humbled by the reality that we don't know everything, that we aren't perfect or all-powerful, and that we don't hold a monopoly on the truth. We should be humbled and awed by the realization that God is at work in other people and creatures in ways that God is not at work in us, that God is revealing things about God's self to others that we cannot imagine. But even as we are humbled by a reckoning with our own limits, we are also invited to be bolstered and amazed by the realization that God is also uniquely at work in us, that God is revealing God's self to us through our own experiences and abilities and understandings—and that we each have that one piece to offer the world. As the lesson of the two pockets tells us, we are but dust and ashes, and yet, for our sake the universe was created.

An oft-told story among LGBTQ Presbyterians is a legend that happens to be true. It is the story of a man named David Sindt, a Presbyterian pastor from Minnesota who was also gay. David became a minister in 1965, when homosexuality was still so staunchly forbidden in the church that the thought of a gay pastor was either an abomination or simply unimaginable. Those who, like David, happened to be both gay and called to ministry were left to persist in quiet secrecy, isolated and deprived of genuine welcome or community, or choose to be open and face rejection by the church. But David could imagine what the church could not. He saw the church's limits as they were, and he knew that there was a world beyond them. And so in 1974, David stood before the Presbyterian General Assembly—the denomination's national gathering—and held up a sign that said, "Is anyone else out there gay?"

This act was the beginning of an organization that eventually became More Light Presbyterians, which is still at work advocating for and supporting LGBTQ members and leaders of the Presbyterian Church. For his efforts, David was forced to leave ministry, and he lived out the remainder of his days as an active lay member of Lincoln Park Presbyterian Church in Chicago. When David died from complications related to AIDS in 1986, the Presbyterian Church was still an institution that limited the participation of LGBTQ people. It still could not imagine a world in which God could call LGBTQ people to lead it in ministry. But decades later, the future that David could imagine did indeed come to be, and I am evidence of it. David knew that the church was limited. He knew that he was limited. But he also knew that God was not, and that knowledge inspired him to dream with God's imagination and plant the seeds to bring that dream into reality.

Sometimes, as in David's story, our faith calls us to imagine beyond the confines of our own limitations or the limitations of our world. At other times, God's creative Spirit turns the very things we see as limitations into gifts in themselves. There is a church called Beacon in the Kensington neighborhood of Philadelphia.[2] It was once a different church. It began in 1871 as a Sunday school mission of First Presbyterian Church of Kensington. From there it grew briefly into its own church before folding in 1879 and then reopening in 1881, eventually calling itself Beacon Presbyterian Church. It moved to the current location, and in the early 1900s it grew expansively alongside the general growth of the neighborhood. It had a large sanctuary, a fellowship hall, and even an education building that briefly housed a college until it burned down in 1920.

Though its numbers diminished, the church survived both the Great Depression and a schism that came at the hands of one of its pastors. In 1954, its beautiful sanctuary was destroyed by Hurricane Hazel. The congregation moved into the fellowship hall, and eventually the damaged sanctuary was demolished and left as a pile of rubble. Over time, Beacon Presbyterian, like Chambers-Wylie in Philadelphia, dwindled in size and was on the verge of dissolution.

Then, in 2011, young ministers from Princeton Theological Seminary came seeking to start a new church development. These ministers got to know their new neighborhood and dreamed about the church that they might build. But the property presented a problem. The old sanctuary had never been rebuilt, and in its place was nothing more than a grassy field. The ministers certainly didn't have the means—financial or otherwise—to build a new sanctuary. But once again the creative Spirit of God was at work.

As the ministers developed relationships with the community around them, they began asking what people really needed from a new ministry there. The answer that came was not a big, shiny sanctuary. Instead, the community talked about how little green space was left in Kensington. What they really needed—what they dreamed of—was a grassy field where their children could safely play. And that, of course, was one thing that the old church already had to offer, thanks to the sanctuary that had been and was no more. Thus, the new worshiping community called Beacon was born. And to this day, the neighborhood meets for worship in the redesigned fellowship hall and for storytelling dinners in the basement that doubles as an art studio for the kids, and children run around and laugh—free, safe, and at home—in the grass where Beacon's sanctuary once stood.

We are limited, but not all in the same way. Our limitations invite us to rely on one another, to connect and share with one another, to push one another and ourselves to creatively become what we might otherwise never have been. We are limited, but God is not. And for a limitless God, even our limits themselves can become holy, beautiful gifts.

# Chapter Eleven

# The Gift of Failure

If you've made it this far in this book, then you already know by the title of this chapter that at some point I'm going to make the claim that there's some redeeming value to be found in failure. In fact, eventually I'm going to argue that failure can be a gift, or at least have gifts to offer us. But not yet. First, I want to say this: I hate failure. I hate it and I'm afraid of it and I have spent most of my life doing everything in my power to avoid it. Of all of the topics I address in this book, it is the one I am least comfortable with, and by a considerable margin. Some of my experiences of failure have been so scarring to me that even years and decades later the memory of them can make my heart clench.

In my experience, there is no other time in life when experiences feel quite as sensitive, desperate, and overwhelming as adolescence. And I suspect that's part of why, after all these years, I still shudder when I think of my elementary-school graduation ceremony. See, we sang a song as part of our graduation, and while most of the song was sung by the whole class, there were two solos—one for a boy and one for a girl. It was the year that the movie *Anastasia* came out, and the song we voted to sing was from that movie, "At the Beginning." Our music teacher announced one week that she would have auditions after school for the solo parts, and anyone was welcome to try out. I knew already, on some level, that I was not a good singer. I'd never

once been told otherwise, and so I'd naturally drawn that conclusion. But I suppose I hoped that it might turn out that I was
wrong. In any case, I had a hard time passing up any opportunity to be center stage, and what's more, I wanted to be the sort
of brave person who would audition for a singing solo without
knowing whether I even stood a chance.

I auditioned. I honestly don't remember much about the experience except that I knew immediately what I'd previously been
only mostly sure about. I was not a singer. Not a good one anyway. Before I'd even finished the song, I knew that there was not
a chance in the world that I would be selected, and I was fairly
embarrassed that I'd even dared to try out and that the handful of
classmates who'd also been at the auditions had heard me.

If the story ended there, I guess it would be a slightly sad,
slightly funny, and fairly standard childhood experience of failure. But that's not where the story ends. The next day, having just
barely begun to recover from the audition experience, I attended
our grade-wide music class, Group Sing. Unexpectedly, in the
final minutes of class, our music teacher announced that there
was a second step to the audition process, and that everyone who
had tried out the day before for her would now audition again—
this time in front of the entire grade.

I can still remember every drop of blood leaving my face. Oh,
how I wish I had been able to simply refuse and withdraw my
name from contention. But I didn't. At my teacher's urging, I
stood up in my place, with one hundred other sweaty, prepubes-
cent sixth-graders staring up at me from where they sat cross-
legged on the ground. And I attempted to sing. I say *attempted*
because I was so afraid and so filled with dread that when my cue
came (or probably not even my cue, if I'm being honest) I opened
my mouth and music did not come out. Sound did, but not song.
A sort of hoarse, strangled version of the words tripped out of my
mouth until the verse ended, and I was mercifully allowed to sit
back down. My classmates cracked up. As for me, "embarrassed"
doesn't come close to describing what I felt. Humiliation maybe.
Mortification, also. But above all—absolute, unbearable shame
about how deeply and publicly I had failed.

I will not attempt to tell you the silver lining of this story. There isn't one—at least not for me. I left that experience without a single positive takeaway, and at least three concrete and deeply rooted fears. First, a fear of public singing. Second, a fear of any kind of unexpected public performance whatsoever. And third, a fear of any activity I didn't know for sure I could succeed at, which is to say—a deep and lasting fear of failure.

I went on to be active in drama club throughout middle and high school, performing in a number of plays, and even minored in theater in college. But from that point forward, I stayed as far from musical theater as I could and avoided anything remotely unscripted. Improv was the bane of my existence—I even hated icebreaker games that put me on the spot in front of a group of people. I generally refused to even go to karaoke nights with friends, and when I did go, I watched and stubbornly refused to participate. There was no exception to this karaoke embargo until nearly twenty years later when I attended a karaoke fund-raiser for the nonprofit arm of the church I worked for in Chicago. I was there as one of two ministers to young adults, many of whom were on the board of the nonprofit and in attendance at the karaoke fund-raiser. I sang. Let's just say I did it for the kids. But I also did it because in that instance, I knew that being unable to sing well would be less of a failure than it would be entertainment for my young adults.

Maybe that experience shook something loose in me, because several months later, when I was looking for some sort of hobby outside ministry, I did the unthinkable: I signed up for improv classes. Despite my fear of unscripted performances, I knew that it was likely to help with my social anxiety and my public speaking, and I knew that it would force me outside of my comfort zone in all sorts of ultimately productive ways. On top of that, I was living in the improv capital of the world—and I knew there'd never be a better time to confront that particular fear. Still, I showed up for my first class filled with dread.

I knew I would make an absolute fool of myself . . . and I did. It helped that everybody else did too, and it also helped that I had an excellent and good-hearted teacher who seemed to approach improv like a ministry in its own right. That first night he addressed the fear of failure—which was palpable in the room—head-on. He said something like, "If you're afraid you're going to fail in this class—let me just go ahead and tell you: you will. Failure is a part of improv, so you might as well go ahead and accept that." And then he said, "But what better place to fail than here—with a community to catch you?" We even played a game in which every time somebody messed up—failed—they had to step forward and bow, while the rest of the class applauded and cheered for them. The goal was to rewire our brain's reaction to failing.

In the end, I found my first class both terrifying and exhilarating. Just before our teacher dismissed us that night, I quipped to a classmate that I'd be fine as long as I didn't have to sing in front of anyone. And, I kid you not, the next thing my teacher told us—to my horror—was that our second week of class would be devoted to musical improv. And it was. A week later, we took turns jumping in front of the whole class to sing a few lines of a song, solo and a cappella, until a teammate would jump in front of us and take it in a different direction. I was terrible, and it was so fun. I did not die. I did not even hate it. The goal wasn't even to be good at singing—it was just to not die from it. To dare to do it and be bad. To play in the face of fear.

My teacher's words and the ethos they spoke to—which played out over and over again during the eight weeks of that class, and the months of more advanced classes after that—utterly shifted my outlook on failure. Certainly, failure isn't the goal of improv. Ideally, an improv show hits all the right notes and unfolds with lots of humor, rhythm, and teamwork. But part of improv is confronting the inevitability of failure, and learning that it is neither fatal nor final.

## "Don't Call It a Failure"
### (How Failure Separates Us)

The best evidence I can offer that we have an unhealthy relationship to failure—besides my own testimony—is what I encountered when I tried to crowdsource stories of failure that led to something positive (an experience of grace, I suggested, or an unexpected outcome, or even just learning). I had my own story of failure and the gifts to be found in it, which I'll get to, but I was hoping for other examples—especially examples that applied to faith communities or group experiences of failure. I tried soliciting responses on Twitter, to no avail. Reaching out to a few friends individually yielded no real stories of failure followed by some kind of positive experience. Finally, feeling a little desperate, I both posted on Facebook and included it in my newsletter, and after all this teeth-pulling, I managed to get a few responses.

Several people talked about being fired from a job. Another couple of people mentioned churches that had closed. And someone else shared an article about a schism that happened in their own church and broader faith community over LGBTQ inclusion. However, the way that people talked about these supposed failures and the way other people responded to them revealed just how uncomfortable we can be with the topic. Those who mentioned losing a job were quick to point out that it was never a good fit in the first place. In response to church closings or divisions, people commented that it's problematic to view those as failures, when in fact they were simply a faithful and prayerfully discerned response to the realities those communities found themselves in. When people were sharing their own stories of failure, they had a tendency to make clear that someone else was responsible. When people were talking about someone's else failures, they rushed to push back on the notion of claiming it as failure at all.

We are really bad at naming failure and owning it for what it is. And when we are able to do that, we are not very good at seeing anything positive about it. Instead, we tend to think back on the experience with some combination of shame and regret. Reflecting on our failures reminds us of our limits and imperfections and humanness. It reminds us that we can screw up in ways that have real and lasting impact and can even hurt people. Essentially, it forces us to reckon with our weaknesses.

Our fear of failure separates us in several different ways. First, we don't like to talk about it. If we are grappling with a failure of our own and the shame and embarrassment that so often come along with that, we're likely to withdraw from others. We do this either so that they won't know that we've failed or because they already know and confronting them also means confronting our failure. Sometimes, our impulse in the face of our own failure is to look for someone or something else to blame, so that it becomes their failure instead of our own.

If we're grappling with someone else's failure, we're also likely to deal with it in one of two ways. First, we reject the person and respond with anger and judgment. Depending on the situation, this response might be entirely valid and even necessary. But it's also likely to either trigger or exacerbate feelings of shame and guilt in the other person, compelling them to withdraw. Alternatively, in seeking to bear grace to others, we might attempt to be comforting or supportive by diminishing the severity of their failure or refusing to name it as such at all. "It's not so bad," we say. The problem here is that, while well-intentioned, we're effectively telling the other person that if it *was* that bad (and sometimes, it really is), it wouldn't be okay. We don't give them a chance to reckon with the full weight of their mistake or their loss while knowing that they are still loved and supported and valued.

Essentially, our inability to name and deal with failure—and especially our inability to recognize the positive possibilities that exist in the presence of failure—further entrenches our fear of it and further compels us to avoid the possibility of failure in all sorts of ways. It makes us hesitant to be vulnerable with one another or express need (because we might get hurt), reluctant to argue too fiercely (because we might lose), afraid of being different (because if we're part of a group, we at least don't have to fail alone), hostile toward both that which troubles us and the protests of others (because they might expose that we are wrong), utterly incapable of withstanding unresolved tension (because as long as it's unresolved, some kind of failure is still a possibility), and desperate to avoid separation (because we view that itself as a failure). At the beginning of this chapter, I confessed that I'm more uncomfortable with failure than any other challenging topic in this book, and I think that's largely because fear of failure drives a lot of our fear of all these other things.

Fear of failure can also make us afraid of one another—especially when we've got different experiences and contexts, different limitations, and different biases. When we don't fully understand one another, being in relationship requires risk. We might not be able to understand, we might offend or hurt, we might do something terribly wrong. I see this in myself and in others, often, when we've tried to engage in some sort of allyship. Being an ally to a population of people who are oppressed in a way that you are not requires trying to recognize realities that are largely invisible to you. And much as in improv, failure is almost guaranteed at one point or another. You're learning and you're doing so in opposition to the narratives and norms around you. At some point, you're likely to screw it up. Our fear of that failure—of being a bad ally—paralyzes us. It makes us afraid to step out and act at all, to speak up or engage. Ironically, the inaction that results from this fear is the fastest way to fail as an ally.

Because we're unwilling to talk about and honestly confront the inevitability of failure, we don't know how to accept it when it happens or receive the gifts it has to offer. Instead we avoid it, hide from it, stick to what we know and are comfortable with, and avoid anyone and anything that brings the possibility of failure to our doorstep.

### The Judas Kiss and How God Shows Up in the Heart of Failure
#### (Failure in the Bible)

People in the Bible screw up a lot. But there are two stories that seem to focus more on failure—and how God responds to failure—than anything else: the story of Jonah and the story of Judas.

Jonah's story doesn't start out being about his own propensity for failure. Instead, it's about the Ninevites who have been screwing up royally for a long, long time. God has had just about enough of their shenanigans, and so God goes to Jonah—who up to this point has apparently been minding his own business—and

God commands Jonah to go to Nineveh and tell the people there that God is going to destroy them all for their wicked ways. This is where the story also becomes about Jonah's failure. The successful response to a call from God would be, "Here I am, Lord. I will go!" But that's not what Jonah says. In fact, he doesn't say anything at all—he just runs in the opposite direction of Nineveh as fast as he can. I'm almost impressed by his audacity. Almost.

Jonah gets to Joppa and buys his way onto a boat headed for Tarshish, "away from the presence of the LORD," he thinks (Jonah 1:3). Unsurprisingly, Jonah also fails to escape from God, who—as we've established—is limitless and everywhere. God causes a mighty storm to rise up around the ship upon which Jonah hides, and his shipmates (in their defense, with his blessing) throw him into the sea, where he is promptly swallowed by a giant fish.

During his three days and nights inside the belly of the fish, Jonah has a profound experience of repentance. He turns back to God, who spares his life and has the fish vomit him back onto dry land. At which point Jonah, having repented, is promptly commanded to do what he has previously failed to do—go to Nineveh and declare their impending doom. This time Jonah goes, and he declares to Nineveh all the ways that they have failed God and how their failures will soon lead to their destruction. The king of Nineveh and his subjects follow Jonah's example and also experience a major moment of repentance, promising to turn over a new leaf in hopes that God will spare them. And God does.

This does not sit well with Jonah, who has just walked all through their city promising their annihilation. Despite the fact that Jonah himself has failed in multiple ways, only to be forgiven and spared by God, he's mad at the thought that God would offer the same deliverance to the Ninevites. In fact, he admits that it wasn't God's wrath or even fear of the Ninevites' wrath that made Jonah run in the beginning, but rather his faith in God's mercy. In Jonah 4:2, after learning of God's plan to spare Nineveh, he says, "O LORD! Is not this what I said while I was still in my own country? That is why I fled to Tarshish at the beginning; for I knew that you are a gracious God and merciful, slow to anger, and abounding in steadfast love, and ready to relent from punishing." Here again, Jonah fails—not in knowing the ways of God, but in trusting them. So God teaches him a lesson. God has a little tree sprout up to protect Jonah from the hot sun that beats down on him outside the walls of Nineveh. And then, in the night, God appoints a worm to eat the tree so that it withers and dies and Jonah is once again exposed. Jonah, overheated and in agony, cries out to God. And God points out that Jonah is weeping and distraught over the loss of this little tree that he had no role in growing and which had come and gone in a single day. How much more then, God explains, is my concern for this city full of people whom I love? And so in Jonah's adventure-packed four chapters, we see that God's response to failure is both the chance to learn and grow, and undeserved grace.

And then there is Judas. The great betrayer, whom Dante sentences to the deepest circle of hell. It's hard to think of a more blatant example of devastating and unforgivable failure than Judas. One of Jesus' closest disciples, one of the Twelve, Judas has been with Jesus since the beginning. And yet on the final night of Jesus' life, Judas hands him over to those who will torture and kill him—and Judas does it all for thirty pieces of silver. Perhaps the most grotesque and painful part of this story is the means by which Judas reveals Jesus to his arresters: with a kiss.

This singular, vile act so thoroughly defines Judas in the Bible that he is hardly ever mentioned apart from his betrayal. In fact, the very first time the disciples are named in the Gospel according to Matthew, Judas is identified as "Judas Iscariot, the one who betrayed him." We've been taught that Judas is evil, but it's hard to grasp the full depth of his failure unless we recognize that to Jesus, Judas was a great deal more than simply his betrayer. Matthew's version of the Last Supper and Jesus' subsequent arrest makes clear that Jesus knows what Judas will do. And long before that it's made clear that Jesus knows that he will die. But it's hard to say at what point Jesus knew the truth about Judas. Maybe he'd always known. Whether he knew or not, Jesus invites Judas in, calls him a dear friend, trusts him, and loves him. Their relationship is real, earnest, deep, storm-weathered, trial-tested, vulnerable, and human. Jesus is not just the Son of God to Judas any more than Judas is just the betrayer to Jesus. They are teacher and student, friends, brothers, family. And it is in this context that Judas hands over Jesus to be killed, kissing him on the cheek and saying, "Greetings, Rabbi!" (Matt. 26:49).

Judas's betrayal—his failure as follower, friend, believer, and human being—is striking in its cruelty and unabashedness. But if there's anything in this story more striking than Judas's act, it's Jesus' response. Because Jesus, knowing full well what this man he loves is doing, receives Judas's kiss and tells him, "Friend, do what you are here to do." Even in this moment of absolute betrayal, Jesus chooses to call Judas *friend*, affirming their relationship and his love for the one who has sold him out. His final message to his beloved disciple, even as he is handed over, is *you are beloved*. Jesus doesn't wait until Judas has realized his error or grappled with his evil or fallen to his knees begging for forgiveness. There is no moment where Christ leaves Judas alone with the weight of his crime.

The tragedy of this story is that Judas cannot feel the love that Jesus offers him. He goes to his grave drowning in the sea of his own brokenness and grief—unable to conceive of any possibility of forgiveness. But there is hope in this story—for us. And if we see it only as a story of failure, we'll miss the gift. It is a story of failure, but it is also a story of love. Of the love God has for us, which is so powerful that it meets us in the very heart of failure and says, "Even here, even here and always, you are loved. Do not be afraid."

## Grace, Growth, and Daring to Do It Afraid
### (How Failure Can Save Us)

This year, I brought home and decorated a live Christmas tree for the first time. I recently moved to Charleston, South Carolina, to be near family and bought my first home, a little condo about six miles from my favorite beach. I think the combination of proximity to family and having a place of my own to decorate put me into Christmas spirit overdrive, so I listened to Christmas music, decorated my house, and watched Christmas movies every day. One movie that keeps coming to mind as I reflect on failure is *It's a Wonderful Life*. It's one of my mom's all-time favorite movies, one of the few that make her tear up, and for years now I've made a point to watch it at least once a Christmas season.

If you're unfamiliar with the classic, it tells the story of George Bailey, a kindhearted man from Bedford Falls, New York, who finds himself, one winter night, desperate enough to want to jump off a bridge. An angel is assigned to intervene, and the first part of the movie consists of scenes from George's life—starting with his childhood—so that the angel can understand how it's come to this. We see young George fiery and full of dreams, bound and determined to get out of Bedford Falls and travel the world. But a series of unforeseen circumstances develop. His father's death leads him to postpone college in order to take over the family business, and then he stays behind and allows his brother to go instead. When his brother returns home from college with a wife and a promising business opportunity, George—who has been waiting for his brother to finally take over the business—lets him go and stays behind again. He marries a girl he's known since childhood, stays behind to care for the town during the war because a childhood injury disqualifies him from service, and struggles to keep his family's loan business afloat despite his absentminded and careless uncle and the town's manipulative and greedy millionaire businessman, Mr. Potter. Finally, when the combined carelessness of Uncle Billy and the manipulations of Mr. Potter cause $8,000 of the Building and Loan company's money to go missing, George finds himself at his wits' end, and on the ledge of a bridge.

What follows, when Clarence the Angel shows up to stop him, is a fantastical journey through a world in which George Bailey had never been born. He's able to see all the good that has come from his life and all the people he has been able to help. He learns that his life has value and returns home to find an entire town ready and willing to help him. The angel's final message to George is this: "No man is a failure who has friends."

It'd be easy to think that this movie shows us how George Bailey thought he had failed, but actually hadn't. But, at the risk of facing public wrath, I'd argue it's not. Failure is, by definition, not accomplishing what one has set out to accomplish. George Bailey fails a lot in his life. He fails to get out of Bedford Falls; he fails to travel the world; in his fear and exhaustion over the missing money, he fails to be a good man to his wife, his children, or his daughter's teacher. The point isn't that he never fails. It's that all the times he has failed don't make *him* a failure. His failures don't define him. In the face of his failures—sometimes even because of them—he achieves other unexpected and unintended successes. He fails and fails, and he succeeds and succeeds, and throughout he strives to live kindly and with love, and that, in the end, is what gives his life meaning. Not the absence of failure, but a richness of life and love that make all the failures worth it.

George's experience, his brush with death, and his reckoning with his losses, enable him to learn about his own value and grow. Often, our failures are also learning experiences. We make the mistake of treating failure like an ending when it is so often the beginning of a new, not yet realized success.

There are also times when the gift to be found in a failure is not so much a particular lesson or a step closer to success, but more an opportunity to encounter grace. That's what I found the summer I lived in Guatemala.

When I was a freshman in college, I made a vow that I would spend my first summer of liberated adulthood doing what I wanted, instead of feeling bound to others' expectations of me. I decided that what I really wanted to do was spend a summer volunteering in another country.

I reached out to a Presbyterian woman in Florida who was a political science professor at a small liberal arts college and had also founded an environmental nongovernmental organization based in Chimaltenengo, Guatemala. The organization was entirely run by Guatemalan employees, but Dr. Anne Hallum went down every summer for a little while and took several students with her. I'd never been to Guatemala, but I knew of Dr. Hallum's work because my church contributed to her organization, the Alliance for International Reforestation (AIR). I convinced Dr. Hallum to let me come down for eleven weeks—six of which would overlap with the visit by her, her husband, and her students. I convinced my church to fund me. I would live with one of AIR's employees, or *técnicos*, and his family, and shadow him in his work. I'd also help Dr. Hallum and her students host the church groups that came down. In preparation, I took a mere one semester of Spanish and read everything I could about Guatemala.

When the day came to leave for Guatemala, I was supposed to meet Dr. Hallum and her students at the Atlanta airport. They were flying up from Florida, and then we were all going to fly down together. They didn't show, and I was so eager to prove myself that I boarded the plane without them, afraid that if I didn't the trip would somehow not happen. It would have been an absolute disaster—I had no cell phone, no contact info, and (remember) only one semester of Spanish—but luckily for me, my companions came pounding down the ramp into the plane at the very last minute.

For a while after that, things ran smoothly. We stayed the first few weeks at a hotel with the professor and her husband and the church groups that came down. I learned about nonprofit management, the devastating realities of deforestation in Guatemala, and the role that corporations like Dole and Del Monte played in that destruction. I went with my *técnico*, Luis, to the villages where he served as liaison, learning about their tree nurseries and the leadership system AIR had set up, about the science behind agroforestry, and how to build environmentally friendly ovens. I also learned a whole lot of Spanish. I learned what it's like to live in a country with a language that you don't fully understand. And, thanks to the language barrier, for the first time in my life I was more inclined to listen than to speak.

It was an adventure, full of learning, challenges, laughter, community, faith experiences, and love. In many ways, it was one of the best experiences of my life. But over time, I began to struggle. Even with all the learning, I didn't know enough of the language to communicate as well as I wanted, I wasn't confident enough to be helpful in the ways I wanted to, and I was lonely. I had been attending sleepaway summer camps since I was six years old, and I had never in my life struggled with homesickness. But suddenly, I missed my family and friends profoundly. I feared the day when the professor and her last student would leave, and I would still have a full month left. In the quiet moments, when I couldn't escape the onslaught of my own thoughts, I knew that what I really and desperately wanted was to go home. But I also knew that would mean admitting failure. I had promised people that I was going to stay for the full summer. I had made commitments. I had convinced Dr. Hallum to take a major risk on me, and I'd convinced my church to pay for it. Both my pride and my deep need to please people shouted at me to suck it up and deal. But I couldn't.

In the final days of Dr. Hallum's time in Guatemala, I shared with her a journal entry about my feelings. I talked about my challenges, but mostly I wrote about missing my family. I had so deeply believed that my future and my success and my destiny were all wrapped up in fearlessly leaving my family behind to go out into the world, and here I was running up against the powerful, painful, and utterly unexpected realization that all I wanted was to make a beeline for the people I loved most.

I gave up. That is the truth. I won't spin it, because there isn't anything to spin. I set out to spend a summer in Guatemala; I made promises about what I would do. And I failed. In the end, I left after seven weeks, a week after Dr. Hallum left, on the same flight as her last student. All these years later, I can conjure now the list of lessons I learned from that experience—both all the good and challenging things that happened during my time in Guate, as we called it, and the failure itself. But for a long time, the only positive thing that came out of my decision to leave (other than the relief I felt reuniting with my family) was that I learned how to confront my own capacity for failure, my own limits, and bear grace to myself and receive it from others.

Dr. Hallum's response to my journal entry was the last one I expected. She wasn't angry or judgmental; she was empathetic. She didn't diminish the weight of what it would mean for me to leave, but she did allow me the space to make the choice with her support. I was similarly surprised by the reactions of my parents and my pastor. Maybe they were disappointed. Or maybe they'd expected it all along and so it wasn't a big deal to them. But all of them, each in their own way, honored the gravity of my struggle and accepted my decision and me with astounding grace. It took me longer—much longer—to find grace for myself. But I did eventually. One day, I came to accept that I was imperfect, that I had failed to keep my promise, failed to fully accomplish what I set out to do—and that none of that diminished my worth. I think that experience, and the journey that followed, was actually the seed that ultimately shifted my relationship to failure and allowed me to risk failure again and again, knowing that even if success didn't find me, grace already had.

What God knows that we so clearly don't is that grace is unconditional. It doesn't depend on avoiding failure, nor does it require that our failures be diminished, denied, or reframed as something else. The grace of God does not deal in spin. Failure, it turns out, is not only neither final nor fatal; it also doesn't separate us—even for a moment—from the love of God. That love stands beside us as we tremble in fear of what we might lose. It takes our hand as we jump into risk. And it waits for us on the other side in success or in failure, unchanged, unwavering, boundless.

This is what I want us to learn. Failure is scary. It's okay to be afraid—but we don't have to be controlled by that fear. We don't have to let it drive us into hiding, away from each other, away from risk, and away from possibility. So often we see conflict as a failure—to love well, to be in community, to embody peace. And in our efforts to avoid reckoning with that failure, we avoid conflict and push each other away, either outright or simply by refusing to engage each other honestly. Conflict may be a failure to maintain perfect harmony, but it isn't a failure of authentic relationship. It's an opportunity to grow. To give and receive grace in the midst of hard things. We are not so gracious as God—none of us. And we can't embody perfect grace the way God can. But we can believe that it exists—for us and for others—and we can try to offer it honestly, without condition or equivocation.

We can risk, and we can screw up entirely. We can own that failure too, and learn from it, and grow, and stretch, and gather our courage, and try again. And fail again. And try again. Even when the lessons are hard to come by, or when they're really hard, even when our failures have serious consequences that we must reckon with, even then there is grace. And opportunity. And possibility for something new and better. At our best, we don't even have to wrestle with this truth alone. We can risk in community, fail in solidarity, grow with each other and from each other. Become better, draw closer. To each other. To God. To the kindom.

Failure is not fatal. It is not final. And it isn't evil either. The promise of God, even in the heart of failure, is this: We are beloved, and we need not be afraid.

# Chapter Twelve

# The Gift of Uncertainty

One of the handful of movies I never seem to grow tired of is *Shakespeare in Love*. A character in the movie, Phillip Henslowe, owns the Rose theater and owes a great deal of money to a lender named Mr. Fennyman, which he promises will come through after the premiere of Shakespeare's new play. When the Master of the Revels shuts down all the theaters before the play opens, Fennyman tracks down Henslowe and threatens him with violence. But Henslowe explains, "The natural condition [of the theater business] is one of insurmountable obstacles on the road to imminent disaster." Fennyman asks, "So what do we do?," and Henslowe tells him, "Nothing. Strangely enough it all turns out well." When Fennyman asks him how, Henslowe pauses and then says, "I don't know. It's a mystery."

How often do we hear someone openly admit that they don't know something? How often do we see someone being perfectly comfortable with the unknown? In my experience, we prefer knowing. We prefer certainty and control and reliability. But the truth is, we live in very uncertain times. Everywhere you look, there are questions without easy answers. What will become of our world in the face of climate change? Will America as we know it even survive the rest of the century? What lasting resolution can be found for the violent conflicts happening around the world? What is to be done about the growing political polarization

189

happening in this country and elsewhere, which seems to be increasingly about dehumanization, hate-fueled rejection, and disengagement rather than earnest difference? Are we doomed? And if so, how soon?

If the Enlightenment was an age of answers, when previously unknown things were rapidly being discovered and understood, it might be fair to say that we live in an age of questions, and we don't even really know how much we don't know.

I believe that, whatever the answers are, we must first accept the reality of our own uncertainty. We do not know. Not everything, not fully. And we must also accept an even harder truth: we may never know. Not in this lifetime.

If you were hoping I was going to end this book with The Answer—the one perfect solution to the divisions and disunity that so define our world these days—I'm here to disappoint you. I'm comfortable saying, like Henslowe, that I don't know. Actually, I don't even believe there is an answer. I don't think there is one perfect, implementable, surefire, certain solution.

I have ideas, obviously. Every chapter of this book suggests a reframing of the way we understand certain challenges so that we might benefit from their gifts, and all of that is rooted in the idea that disunity itself may not be so much a problem to be solved as a holy opportunity for growth and transformation. Disunity is so often seen as an evil: the breakdown of relationship, of community, of cohesion. But disunity doesn't have to mean destruction. In the arguments and protests born from our disunified state, we hear hard but important truths that push back on our assumptions and our hubris. In our willingness to confront our own doubts, and others', about things we've always assumed to be true, we are invited to discover new and deeper understandings of truth. In disunity, our differences and limitations and failures clash against one another, sometimes violently, but those clashes can also be an invitation for us to be stretched and expanded—or at least to understand that the world and humanity are more expansive than any one of us. Our hunger can turn us into enemies, seeking to deprive one another so that we ourselves might have enough. But our hunger also reminds us that we need more than ourselves;

we are not sufficient alone. And even when our disunity puts us utterly and irrevocably at odds, when it demands that we be separate, that gulf between us offers space for each of us to grow—perhaps even toward each other.

Disunity is tense. But in that tension we catch a glimpse of the wondrous complexity of God and God's creation. The universe is made up of an infinite chorus of voices, and we have been taught to see the beauty of harmony, all those voices aligned. But there is beauty in cacophony as well—and it is the beauty of hearing just how many voices there are, of realizing that humanity and God's good creation do not always look like us or even like what we understand. Embracing the holiness of disunity doesn't mean seeing beauty or purpose in every opinion or argument; it means seeing that there is beauty and purpose in every person and maybe in the discord itself. Disunity is stretching us, pushing us—both together and apart, refining us, and along with all the other holy work of God, making something new. Even in the negative space between us, God is making new creation. And because God is there working in the negative space even as God is at work in us, we are still all bound up together in God, and even in our disunity we are, somehow, connected to one another.

I believe the disunity we find ourselves in has the power to save us, if we listen to it and learn from it and allow ourselves to be transformed by it. But this journey toward discovering and embracing the unexpected gifts found in disunity—this path of transformation—is itself full of uncertainty. It isn't straightforward, or crystal clear, or universal. Some of these gifts offer a path forward for certain contexts and situations, but not others. And others of these gifts may offer answers in different moments and scenarios. The uncertainty of it all can be frustrating and scary.

But believe it or not, uncertainty has its own role to play and its own gifts to offer if we open ourselves to it. One of our biggest mistakes is believing that our unknowing, our uncertainty, is something we're supposed to "fix." Our task is not to solve it. Our task is to accept it and figure out what it means to live with it. To do this requires something, and that thing it requires is also the very gift it offers: faith.

### The Illusion of Certainty and What It Costs Us

In a letter he wrote when he was only twenty-eight years old, German author and thinker Rainer Maria Rilke suggested that we're not actually meant to concern ourselves with answers. He says,

> Have patience with everything unresolved in your heart and to try to love the questions themselves as if they were locked rooms or books written in a very foreign language. Don't search for the answers, which could not be given to you now, because you would not be able to live them. And the point is, to live everything. Live the questions now. Perhaps then, someday far in the future, you will gradually, without even noticing it, live your way into the answer.[1]

It's a thoughtful sentiment, but a dreadfully difficult instruction to follow. Our instincts drive us to seek control, safety, security—questions without answers do none of that. Instead they remind us that we don't have full control, that we're not entirely safe or secure. In the absence of certainty, we create an illusion of it by adhering to dogmatic convictions as if they are fact rather than belief. We cast out anyone who pokes holes in our dogma or suggests that we might be wrong. We draw hard lines in the sand to cut ourselves off from others whose "certainty" opposes ours. We defend our convictions (to others or just to ourselves) by saying "I just know" rather than naming it as belief. We equate certainty with faithfulness, when in fact, as my classmate Gordon reminded me years ago, certainty not only isn't the same thing as faith, it is actually faith's opposite. If you know something with absolute certainty, you cannot choose to believe and trust in that belief.

Doubt and uncertainty are closely related, but they're not exactly the same thing either, at least not as I use the words here. Doubt tends to be a momentary questioning of what one otherwise feels fairly sure about. On the other side of doubt is either a return to one's belief or a shift to a different belief that one doesn't feel doubtful about. Uncertainty is a lingering acknowledgment of not knowing or fully understanding. It's perhaps the marriage of doubt and unresolved tension. Doubt might best be understood as the doorway between our uncertainty and our belief.

One of the most significant and counterproductive phantoms I see us construct in our fearful flight from uncertainty is what I call the myth of arriving. We operate as though it's possible to get to some static point of resolution. We plan and debate as if, at some point in this life and this world, we can reach an ending, where problems have all been solved and everything presumably stays happy and perfect forever. In fact, I often hear and see people acting as though we are meant to operate this way—especially Christians.

More than anywhere else, I see this at play in conversations about unity. As I've mentioned elsewhere, Christians—primarily moderates, but not always—contend that we are called to unity above all else. They point to Scriptures that call for being "of the same mind" and living together in harmony, and especially to the theological claim that we are all made one in Christ. I absolutely believe that we are all bound up together in the love of God and in Christ. But the unity and peace that Christ calls for are a perfect unity and a perfect peace that are aligned with perfect justice, mercy, kindness, and understanding. That kind of unity has never been created by humanity in this world because neither this world nor any of us is perfect. We are flawed, fragile, and broken creatures. Perfect unity is beyond our power to create or destroy, and we will only truly understand it and live into it in the world yet to come.

When we believe that holy unity is not only within our capacity, but is in fact our responsibility to create, we are buying into the myth of arriving. It is not our task in this life to arrive at a certain point or place. Our task is to understand and accept that we won't—not in this life. And not through our own power. The convictions that divide us are fueled by questions that we cannot know the answers to yet, and so we are left to choose what we believe and fight for that belief. In the absence of absolute certainty, we are bound to a reality of relative unrest. And that is *okay*.

Too often when we make the mistake of thinking we can arrive, we settle for half measures and false certainties. When it comes to our dogged pursuit of unity, the cost is usually justice and respect and even relationship itself. When we call for unity first and above all, we try to construct a unity that is not based on genuine understanding, trust, or mutual recognition of people's God-belovedness. It's based on fear of conflict and desperation, and it almost always requires that some people be silenced, that some people settle for only a superficial inclusion that is tense and conditional. We may indeed have it within our power to create that sort of unity, but I don't think there's a single ounce of holiness in it.

I rather think we are called to consider that for a boundless, creative, and loving God, even disunity can have a holy purpose, and our work is to faithfully lean in and learn from it.

## How to Live in a Postascension World
### (Uncertainty in the Bible)

Even Jesus understands that part of faith is making peace with uncertainty. When Nicodemus peppers him with logistical questions after Jesus says a person must be "born from above," Jesus replies, "The wind blows where it chooses, and you hear the sound of it, but you do not know where it comes from or where it goes. So it is with everyone who is born of the Spirit" (John 3:8). It's not the most easily unpacked answer, but what seems clear is that Jesus is telling Nicodemus, "There are some things you're just not going to fully understand, but you can still believe and trust in them." He goes on to speak about how we testify based on what know and understand, and that from those earthly, known things, we can come to have faith in heavenly things, even those beyond our comprehension. There's something comforting in that message—that we can have faith *seeking* understanding, as Anselm said, and that we don't need to totally understand in order to have faith.

My theology professor in seminary once told us a story about Madeleine L'Engle, a writer of both children's fantasy novels and Christian thought. After a public talk by the author, during a time for questions from the audience, a young girl stood up. She told L'Engle that she had read *A Wrinkle in Time*. L'Engle was impressed because the girl was so young. She asked, "Did you understand it?" And the girl thought for a minute before responding, "I didn't understand it, but I knew what it was about." Jesus' advice to us about how to live in the face of inevitable uncertainty is similar. We can know without knowing. We can trust what it's about without fully understanding.

This is good news for us, caught as we are in the space between Christ's living on earth and his coming again. Not long ago I had the opportunity to guest preach on Ascension Sunday. I had never spent a whole lot of time thinking about the ascension as an experience or what its impact might have been on Jesus' followers, but this time around my encounter with their story really struck a chord. These folks have been following Jesus for three years. They have listened to and learned from his teachings. They've asked questions when they didn't understand. They've loved him. And they've already lost him once. They've suffered through the debilitating grief of the tomb and rejoiced at the startling revelation of the resurrection. And no doubt, they clung all the more tightly to Jesus after that.

Now, here he is, blessing them and offering one more round of advice, telling them to stay in Jerusalem and wait on the promise of the Father (that is, the Spirit who will come to them at Pentecost), and then go out in the world proclaiming forgiveness and repentance to all people in his name (Luke 24:36–53). And right in the middle of this grand speech, when he is still talking to them, he is raised up into the sky and spirited away from them forever—or at least until the kingdom comes. They have been, once again, left behind.

We don't talk much about this postascension time. It's a sort of in-between period, when the story of Jesus' life on earth has ended, and a new story—of the church, which will begin at Pentecost—hasn't yet begun. There's no script for these moments, no stage directions, no clear-cut steps to take, no certainty. And even when the Spirit does come at Pentecost to accompany and guide them out into the world, they are still living in something of an in-between time. The days of Jesus teaching them exactly what to do and clarifying when they do not understand are over. He is gone. And they have been promised that a new world is coming, and soon, but time stretches on and on and their lives dwindle, and then other lives, and then others, and still the soon-to-be-born new creation doesn't come. Christ still does not return.

In the absence of Jesus, the disciples try their best to follow his advice, trusting in the Holy Spirit and taking the gospel out into the world. In the face of new questions and challenges, they trust in what they know of who Christ was and is and do what they can to live out his teachings in new and ever-evolving ways for a new and ever-evolving world. Sometimes it leads them to surprising places and unorthodox decisions.

In Acts 8:26–39, we learn the story of Philip, who runs into an angel and is told to go to a road from Jerusalem down to Gaza. The author of Acts makes a point of saying that "this is a wilderness road," conjuring images of untamed brush and a dusty, rarely traveled path. Philip, being obedient, does indeed go, and on this road in the middle of nowhere he encounters an Ethiopian eunuch, a court official for Queen Candace of Ethiopia, riding by in his splendid chariot. Philip hears the eunuch reading from Isaiah, so he runs up to the chariot and asks, "Do you understand what you are reading?" To which the man replies, "How can I, unless someone guides me?" So Philip joins him in the chariot and they read together and Philip teaches him about Jesus. And then, suddenly, they come upon some water and the eunuch asks, "What is to prevent me from being baptized?"

"Wilderness" is a loaded term in the Bible. It's an unfamiliar and unknown place, an undefined and unruly space. Here on this wilderness road, in a postascension world that is something of a wilderness in its own right, Philip and this eunuch—who are both far outside their contexts and comfort zones—encounter each other in an unexpected way. And Philip is confronted with a question. The eunuch wants to be baptized, and Philip is the one to do it. The thing is, when the man asks, "What is to prevent me from being baptized?" the answer is not "Nothing." In those days, the real answer was a variety of purity codes and regulations. Had they been in Jerusalem it probably wouldn't have happened. But instead they find each other in the wilderness, where nothing is quite so black-and-white or certain. So Philip makes a choice. He chooses to live out the promise of Jesus' radically inclusive love in a new way and offers a different response to the eunuch's question. What is to prevent him from being baptized? Nothing at all.

The eunuch is baptized, the love of Christ is shared, and the two men part ways as family and brothers rather than strangers. Maybe uncertainty and wilderness aren't always bad things; maybe sometimes they are the inspiration for new possibilities and unexpectedly beautiful ways to live out the questions we confront.

We are still living in that in-between time. The world is a wilderness, and these days, that's not hard to believe. It's common parlance among many of my preacher friends to say that we are "Easter people living in a Good Friday world"—and in these troubled times that certainly has some resonance. But what we actually are is Easter people living in a postascension world, and that is a struggle all its own. We have our Holy Scriptures, we have the Holy Spirit, and we have teachings and traditions passed down through the ages. But every day brings new life, new and unexpected realities, and challenges, and questions. And we are left to muddle through as best we can, without knowing for certain what the right path is, what the right answers are, what Jesus would say or do. Like the disciples in those first unscripted days, we have to make peace with our uncertainty, trust in what we do know, and have faith in what can be.

### What a Little Bird (and BeBe) Told Me about Embracing Uncertainty

When you are a queer person pursuing ministry in a denomination that only recently decided to believe God can call LGBTQ people, you spend a lot of time trying to convince people that you deserve to belong. That you are qualified, worthy, and called to be ordained. You can't waver at all because all around you are people who are just waiting for a reason to doubt you and disqualify you. You spend years trying to prove how certain you are that you should be a minister, and you never have a second to question it yourself. After a while, it starts to seem like the perfect happy ending, if you can just be lucky enough to get it. At least, that's how it felt for me.

After seminary, I landed an amazing job as a pastoral resident at a large downtown church in Chicago. I was ordained on November 15, 2014, in a worship service I designed, which took place at the church that had become my home community in Austin. My friend John, who had become the first openly gay man ordained in our denomination in Texas exactly one year before, preached a sermon about Queen Vashti. My youth pastor whom I'd known since age eight gave me my charge. My dad sat in the front row. My mom read Scripture and draped my first stole over my shoulders. My friends cheered and cried. We sang all my favorite hymns. And I broke bread and presided at the Communion table for the first time. It was a beautiful, almost perfect, storybook kind of day.

After it was over, I flew back to Chicago to continue my first ministry job. However much I had come to believe that ordination to ministry was my happy ending, and however much my ordination service felt like a fairy tale—ministry, it turned out, is not a fairy tale. Nor is it an ending, happy or otherwise. It's a job. And it is *hard*. I struggled a lot during those two years as a pastoral resident, even though I loved the people and I loved preaching, teaching, and leading worship. I often felt uncertain about whether I was really called to ministry, and if so, to what specific ministries I was called. But I was afraid to admit it because I'd fought so hard to get there and because in general we act as though pastors should never experience uncertainty and because I'm just as uncomfortable with uncertainty as the next person.

After my residency was over, I moved to Washington, DC, to seek out work in a faith-based advocacy organization, and ended up being hired at *Sojourners*. I'm still ordained, most days I still feel called to ministry of some sort, and always, I am still uncertain about it—about what it means or what it should look like or how to move forward. I'm not entirely comfortable living with uncertainty, but I am slowly learning how.

Last year, when I traveled to Northern Ireland to work on my story about Corrymeela, I spent my first few days in Belfast, staying with friends and interviewing people from the Catholic and Presbyterian churches I was writing about. After that, I rented a car and spent the rest of my time staying at an Airbnb home on the northern coast. It was my second trip to Northern Ireland, and the gorgeous rocky coastline and deep blue water were a balm to my soul. I'd arrived carrying heaviness inside me. I was grieving the loss of a relationship that had been new but seemed promising. I was struggling with major unknowns in life—would I ever find someone, would I ever have children, should I move home, and, as ever, what am I called to do? I was frustrated that every attempt I'd made to find success or answers to some of these questions had backfired, but on some level I also knew that I needed to learn how to accept that I couldn't know everything and I couldn't control everything. I felt a little bitter and snarky about it, though, so I had decided that my mantra was going to be "give up." I even had it printed on a copper bracelet.

My days on the coast were beautiful, quiet, soulful, and relaxing, but they didn't exactly hand-deliver the peace of mind I was looking for. And then, late on my last night, I heard two women downstairs who had apparently just arrived at the Airbnb house. I walked down and met Bird and BeBe, who were several decades older than me and had been traveling together all around the British Isles. They shrieked when they heard me say "y'all," and it turned out they were from Texas, where I had spent six years in my twenties working and going to grad school. It was powerful to hear the familiar accent when I was halfway around the world, and their spirited and lively natures were infectious. We hit it off immediately, but I was tired and planning to get up early to leave, so after a brief conversation I said good night and headed to bed, thinking that I wouldn't see them again.

The next morning, before I set out to drive down the coast and then back to Belfast, I took one last walk down to the beach to watch the sun rise over the waves and pray again for peace and the courage to "give up." When I came back to the house, BeBe and Bird were just sitting down to breakfast. They invited me to join them, and even though I was eager to get on the road, I sat down at their table. Over several cups of coffee, with lots of laughter, they took turns telling me the story of how they had spent four years planning out every last detail of this three-week trip they were on. The whole point of their journey was to arrive at a place called the Callanish Stones—an ancient ring of rocks sort of like Stonehenge—on a tiny, remote island off the coast of Scotland at precisely 9:02 p.m. on the autumnal equinox. I don't entirely remember what was supposed to happen, but it was clear that it was very important to them.

From the moment they arrived, their plans began to fall apart. Missed reservations, the challenge of driving a rented car where everything is on the opposite side, bad luck. BeBe and Bird were remarkably joyous as they described the amazing and frustrating combination of misfortunes that had befallen them.

Despite all that had gone wrong, the two women kept trying to make it to their destination, until eventually, an issue with a train schedule made it clear to them that there was no way they would get to the stones by 9:02.

"We just had to surrender," BeBe said to me. "We had to accept that we weren't going to make it."

"Sometimes," Bird said, "you have to give up, and then see what happens."

And so they did. They gave up. And somehow—by incredible circumstance—they arrived at their inn on the small island with five minutes to spare and found two Canadians headed to the stones who offered them a ride. They left their bags in the road and got in. When they arrived, they found two other strangers, Scotsmen, one of whom was wearing a black hoodie and drinking a beer, and he pulled out some bagpipes and played them as the group of six strangers made their way up to the stones and stood together at precisely 9:02 p.m. on the autumnal equinox.

At the end of their story, my eyes were wide and I told them, "You're not going to believe this, but I came on this trip exactly because I needed to learn this lesson about surrender and trust."

Bird said, "Oh, of course I believe it. This is the universe at work too, you see."

Bird and BeBe knew something about learning to live with uncertainty and learning to let go and have faith in the universe. They also knew that beautiful stories can be born from uncertain moments. They helped me to learn it too.

### Living Out Faith in an Uncertain World
#### (How Uncertainty Can Save Us)

Of course, it's not enough just to surrender and accept uncertainty. Despite my snark, I know that we can't just give up. As people of faith, in particular, we are called to show up and live and love and serve in this world—even if we don't always have the answers about how.

In the wake of the 2016 election, a pastor friend of mine wrote about how polarized the campaign season had been, and how much more polarized things had felt *after* the election, and how uncertain everyone was feeling about how to live in this hard new reality. He suggested that it was time for Presbyterian faith leaders to write a new statement of faith that was specifically crafted to suggest how we ought to respond faithfully in times like these. I was invited to be a part of a team of eight faith leaders—six of us to write a statement, and two to support us. We were a group with many different stories, contexts, and perspectives. Two of us were out and queer, half of us were women, there was a black man and an Asian American woman; I was the youngest, at thirty, and the oldest were in their fifties. We were all ordained, but I was working as a journalist, another writer was a theology professor at the seminary I attended, another was serving as a pastor in a different denomination. We shared a common commitment to trying to embody the grace and love of Christ in this world, but we didn't exactly agree about what that meant or how it should look.

We all deeply believed, however, that we ought to try to figure out what a faithful response would look like in our troubled modern context. We gathered in person for one twenty-four-hour period, and then spent weeks honing our document via Skype calls and emails and Google docs. We argued and debated and pushed one another and ourselves, and we produced a document that we named after the place where it had been born: the Sarasota Statement.[2] We aimed to make it a challenging and convicting read for Christians of various beliefs and contexts, an "equal opportunity squirmer," as I liked to call it.

The final statement laments the ways that we rejected, demonized, and dehumanized others; condoned violence and oppression; failed to offer hospitality and true welcome; and remained complacent and silent in the face of injustice. It reaffirms belief in a Jesus who welcomed all, loved all, and rejected violence, injustice, and tyranny in every form, choosing relationship and mercy instead. The statement also declares our commitment to striving in every possible way to live out the ideals that Jesus embodied and taught, rejecting and fighting against any earthly reality that undermines love and grace. In our preamble, we admit that "we believe God's Kingdom comes not because we are confident in our own capacities, but because we trust in God, who can do more than we can ask or imagine." But we also say that even if God's kingdom (or kindom, as I prefer) cannot exist in this world and life, we are still invited to help it draw nearer in whatever ways we can. In our closing, we acknowledge that being human and living in an uncertain and broken world means constantly reexamining and recommitting our efforts, saying, "We commit to continuously rededicate ourselves to this work and strive, with hearty faith, to live this Kingdom on earth."

The Sarasota Statement is an imperfect document because it was written by imperfect people. But I'm proud of it and proud to have been a part of creating it, because I believe it is an example of how we can go about making our best efforts to be faithful in the face of uncertainty. We do it through relationship, through struggle, and sometimes even through conflict. We do it by acknowledging our limitations and our vulnerability, and by taking responsibility for where we've failed. We do it by trying, and then getting it wrong, and trying again, learning and growing in grace. We do it by recognizing that we will never quite "get there"—not in this lifetime, but that the Holy Spirit is with us and around us and at work in us as we make our best efforts. Faithfully living in the already/not yet of an uncertain, imperfect, postascension world means continuing ever onward toward the world of God's promise, finding peace and beauty in the journey itself, and never ever settling for less—not for half measures, hollow attempts at approximating the peace and unity that comes from God, or idolatrous and hubristic worship of what we ourselves create.

There is a famous prayer often attributed to Archbishop Oscar Romero, though it was actually written by Bishop Ken Untener for a homily given by Cardinal John Dearden in 1979. It says, "It helps, now and then, to step back and take a long view. The kingdom is not only beyond our efforts, it is even beyond our vision. We accomplish in our lifetime only a tiny fraction of the magnificent enterprise that is God's work. Nothing we do is complete, which is a way of saying that the Kingdom always lies beyond us."[3] But he went on to say,

> We cannot do everything, and there is a sense of liberation in realizing that. This enables us to do something, and to do it very well. It may be incomplete, but it is a beginning, a step along the way, an opportunity for the Lord's grace to enter and do the rest. We may never see the end results, but that is the difference between the master builder and the worker. We are workers, not master builders; ministers, not messiahs. We are prophets of a future not our own.

We are indeed prophets of a future not our own. And we are prophets who cannot see the full scope of the very truth we aim to speak and live out. We are living in a world of uncertainty even as we were made for a world of certain, perfect goodness, unity, and peace. We don't have to understand it to know what it's about. We don't have to be certain to have faith and try our best to live it out. We can trust that God is at work—not just in the world to come, but right here and now. Right in the middle of this broken world, God is at work making new creation out of chaos. God is at work even in disunity itself, doing something mysterious and holy. And God is daring us to join in. We don't have to know. We just have to believe.

# Questions for Reflection and Discussion

### Chapter 1: The Gift of Difference

1. Why do you think God made creation with so much diversity?

2. In what ways are you different from others? What is a formative experience of difference you've had? How do you feel about these differences?

3. What gifts have you encountered in others because they are different from you?

4. What challenges have you faced in interacting with others because of ways they are different from you? Can you identify any positives in this experience?

5. Why do you think people are afraid of difference? How does this fear impact the world? How might it be overcome?

6. How might individual or interpersonal experiences of difference function differently than our experiences of difference between large groups of people, based on race, politics, religion, and so on?

## Chapter 2: The Gift of Doubt

1. Do you believe that Jesus experienced doubt? Why or why not? How is his doubt, or lack thereof, important to your faith?

2. How do you believe God feels about doubt?

3. Where do you encounter doubt most in your life? Where in your faith?

4. Can you think of a time when doubt separated you from someone else or caused conflict? Was there a time when doubt opened a new door of discovery for you?

5. In what negative ways do you see doubt impacting our world and society? In what positive ways do you think doubt has (or could have) an impact on our world and society?

6. What do you think would happen if we embraced doubt in the places where it scares us or feels threatening? Would any good potentially come from it?

## Chapter 3: The Gift of Argument

1. What do you think God would have done if Abraham had argued with him about Isaac? Why do you think Jesus let the Syrophoenician woman argue with him?

2. What were you taught or shown about argument as a child? Do you tend to get into arguments or avoid them?

3. Do you believe that argument can be a gift? Why or why not? What are the qualities of a good (that is, productive or helpful) argument?

4. Think of the worst argument you can remember being in or witnessing. What made it terrible? Have you ever had something positive grow out of an argument?

5. How have you seen the church handle intense argument? Is this good or bad? What might be a better way?

6. What do you think would happen if we set aside civility and allowed for frank, impassioned argument? Is there a way to do this well?

## Chapter 4: The Gift of Tension

1. Where in the Bible do you see people struggling with tension between God's call and their life circumstances? Or with situations that have no easy answer? How do they deal with that tension? How does God deal with that tension?

2. Can you think of a time in your life when you recognized that there was not an easy resolution or black-and-white answer? How did you handle that?

3. Have you heard people use the phrase "live in the tension"? What does this phrase mean to you?

4. In what ways does our faith require us to make peace with unresolved tension?

5. Where have you seen black-and-white, either-or thinking amplify conflict? Was the either-or framing accurate and necessary, or were things actually more nuanced?

6. How might embracing nuance and accepting ongoing unresolved tension transform some of the current conflicts in your life and community, in the church, and in the world?

## Chapter 5: The Gift of Separation

1. Where do you see separation function in a positive way in the Bible?

2. Where have you seen or experienced separation as a negative thing to be avoided? Did anything good come out of it?

3. Can you think of a time when you experienced a separation as a primarily positive experience? Why was it positive for you?

4. Do you believe that separation is ever necessary? Why and when, or why not?

5. Why do you think we are so fearful of separation?

6. Can separation ever be helpful in healing conflict? How? Do you think separation can be good even if it doesn't lead to reconciliation? Why or why not?

## Chapter 6: The Gift of Vulnerability

1. What have you been taught about vulnerability? Have you been taught to embrace it or avoid it? Why?

2. Have you ever experienced vulnerability (yours or someone else's) in a negative way? What was negative about it? What risks and challenges exist in being vulnerable?

3. Think of with whom or where in your life you can be vulnerable. Why do you feel comfortable there or with them? Who feels comfortable being vulnerable with you? Why?

4. How have you seen vulnerability used against people (either individually or systemically)? Have you seen it divide people? Bring people together? How?

5. How can the practice of mutual vulnerability transform the way we approach people we disagree with? How might it change the way we think about the things that divide us?

6. How might the church help create spaces for people to be mutually vulnerable?

## Chapter 7: The Gift of Trouble

1. In what ways do you see Jesus "stirring things up" in the Gospels? How does he respond when he encounters troubling things?

2. What troubles you in the world today? Why?

3. How do you respond when you encounter troubling things? How do you see others respond to troubling things?

4. How often does church make you feel comfortable? How often does it discomfort you? Do you think it's more important for church to comfort people or discomfort them? Why?

5. How have you seen troubling things add to conflict and separate people in the world today?

6. What does it mean to faithfully confront what troubles us? How can it help us deal with conflict? How can the church be helpful in this effort?

## Chapter 8: The Gift of Protest

1. Do you believe that it's okay to protest against God? Do you believe Jesus engaged in protest during his life and ministry? How?

2. Do you believe our faith requires us to protest at times? When and why or why not?

3. Is there a good kind of protest and a bad kind of protest? What is the difference between them? What makes one protest bad and another good?

4. Are there value and importance to protest even if the desired change cannot be achieved? What are the value and importance?

5. What is the faithful way to respond to protests you disagree with?

6. How have you seen protests contribute to division? How have you seen protests lead to good change? How have you seen protests bring people together across differences?

## Chapter 9: The Gift of Hunger

1. How do you think the five loaves and two fish yielded twelve baskets of leftovers? What do you think became of those leftovers? What does this story teach us about hunger, fear of scarcity, and abundance?

2. What does it feel like when you have a need (whether hunger for sustenance or something else) that you are afraid cannot be met? What do you do in response to this fear?

3. How have you seen a fear of scarcity play out in your own life? In the church? In the world?

4. What was special about the way Jesus brought people together over food? In what way do hunger and sustenance bring us together today?

5. What does it mean to come to the table in the midst of conflict? Does our belief in the Table (that is, God's Table) require us to always come to the table (that is, place of shared discussion) with each other in the midst of conflict and division?

6. How can our hunger offer us hope or goodness even when we are not at the table together?

## Chapter 10: The Gift of Limitations

1. How do you think Paul knew to trust Lydia? What do you think would have happened if Eli hadn't been there to tell Samuel that he was hearing the Lord's voice?

2. Where have you run up against your own limitations—in understanding, in experience, in ability? How have others helped you? Where have you been able to help others in the face of their own limitations?

3. How do limitations contribute to bias and misunderstanding? How does a culture of perfectionism, self-sufficiency, and supremacy make us afraid of our limitations?

4. Why do you think we have a tendency to surround ourselves with those who share our particular (limited) perspectives, experiences, and abilities?

5. What does the church have to say about limitations? How does this help or hinder an acceptance of limitations and the gift that may lie in accepting them?

6. What would it take for us, all of us, to collectively acknowledge our limitations? What would happen as a result?

## Chapter 11: The Gift of Failure

1. Why do you think Jonah is so frustrated that God spares the Ninevites, when he himself failed and received God's forgiveness? Do you think God forgives Judas? How do you think God feels about failure? Why is grace sometimes so hard to receive or give?

2. How would you define failure? Where does this understanding come from?

3. Think of a time when you have failed. How did others respond to your failure? How did you respond? How have you responded to others' failures? Did these responses enhance or damage your relationship?

4. Can you think of a time when you, by definition, failed but didn't think of it as a failure? How did you think of it instead? Why did it matter to you to think of it this way, instead of as failure?

5. How do you think failure (and our fear of it) contributes to the ongoing divisions in the world today?

6. What might help us—both individually and collectively—to risk failure or to confront and reckon with our failures?

## Chapter 12: The Gift of Uncertainty

1. Do you believe Jesus experienced uncertainty? What do you think God expects us to do when we feel uncertain about how best to live out our faith?

2. Have you experienced a time when you were certain about something and it turned out not to be true? What made you certain? How did you feel on finding out you were wrong?

3. What do you feel uncertain about today? In your life? In the world? How do you cope with that uncertainty?

4. Why do you think we are so fearful of uncertainty? Why do we choose false certainty instead? What damage comes as a result of this?

5. How does uncertainty—or our fear and avoidance of it—contribute to division and conflict?

6. What might happen if we chose to see uncertainty as a good thing, or at least not inherently bad? What positives might grow out of embracing uncertainty?

# Notes

## Chapter 1: The Gift of Difference

1. The Enneagram Institute, http://www.enneagraminstitute.com/.
2. A shooting at a music festival in Las Vegas on October 1, 2017, killed fifty-eight people, surpassing the death toll of the Pulse nightclub massacre to become the deadliest shooting in modern US history.
3. Ellen Berrey, "Diversity Is for White People: The Big Lie behind a Well-Intended Word," Salon, October 26, 2015, https://www.salon.com /2015/10/26/diversity_is_for_white_people_the_big_lie_behind_a_well_intended_word/.

## Chapter 2: The Gift of Doubt

1. Frederick Buechner, quoted in "Weekly Sermon Illustration: Thomas," *Frederick Buechner Center* (blog), April 2, 2018, http://www.frederickbuechner .com/blog/2018/4/2/weekly-sermon-illustration-thomas.
2. Greg Morse, "Does Your Doubt Dishonor God? What No One Says about Weak Faith," Desiring God, January 4, 2018, https://www.desiringgod.org /articles/does-your-doubt-dishonor-god.
3. Daniel José Camacho, "Why the Religious Left Is a Political Failure," ABC Religion and Ethics, February 1, 2018, http://www.abc.net.au/religion /articles/2018/02/01/4797159.htm.
4. Jerry L. Van Marter, "Austin Seminary Backs Columbia Seminary Statement on Schism," Presbyterian Church (U.S.A.), May 22, 2014, https:// www.pcusa.org/news/2014/5/22/austin-seminary-backs-columbia-seminary -statement-/.
5. More specifically, the polity around ordination in our *Book of Order* removed the "chastity clause," which held that all ordained ministers must practice chastity in singleness or fidelity in marriage. It left regional governing groups and individual congregations the authority to allow or deny ordination of LGBTQ persons as a matter of "freedom of conscience."

## Chapter 3: The Gift of Argument

1. Celeste Ng, *Everything I Never Told You* (New York: Penguin Books, 2015), 161.
2. Online Etymology Dictionary, s.v. "civility (n.)," accessed January 9, 2019, https://www.etymonline.com/word/civility.
3. Dictionary.com, s.v. "civility," accessed January 9, 2019, https://www.dictionary.com/browse/civility.
4. Online Etymology Dictionary, s.v. "polite (adj.)," accessed January 9, 2019, https://www.etymonline.com/word/polite.
5. Callum Borchers. "Trump Says the Media Unfairly Portrays Him as Uncivil, Which He's Not Because He 'Went to an Ivy League College,'" *Washington Post*, October 25, 2017, https://www.washingtonpost.com/news/the-fix/wp/2017/10/25/trump-says-the-media-unfairly-portrays-him-as-uncivil-which-hes-not-because-he-went-to-an-ivy-league-college/.
6. Avi Selk and Sarah Murray. "The Owner of the Red Hen Explains Why She Asked Sarah Huckabee Sanders to Leave," *Washington Post*, June 25, 2018, https://www.washingtonpost.com/news/local/wp/2018/06/23/why-a-small-town-restaurant-owner-asked-sarah-huckabee-sanders-to-leave-and-would-do-it-again/.
7. Mary Jordan, "The Latest Sign of Political Divide: Shaming and Shunning Public Officials," *Washington Post*, June 24, 2018, https://www.washingtonpost.com/politics/the-latest-sign-of-political-divide-shaming-and-shunning-public-officials/2018/06/24/9a29f00a-77bc-11e8-aeee-4d04c8ac6158_story.html.
8. Annie Geng, "Woman Confronts Scott Pruitt at a Restaurant, Urges Him to Resign," CNN, July 3, 2018, https://www.cnn.com/2018/07/03/politics/scott-pruitt-mom-restaurant-confrontation/index.html.
9. Samuel Chamberlain, "Scott Pruitt Resigns as EPA Chief, Trump Announces," Fox News, July 5, 2018, http://www.foxnews.com/politics/2018/07/05/scott-pruitt-resigns-as-epa-chief-trump-announces.html.
10. Michelle Goldberg, "We Have a Crisis of Democracy, Not Manners," *New York Times*, June 25, 2018, https://www.nytimes.com/2018/06/25/opinion/trump-sarah-huckabee-sanders-restaurant-civility.html.
11. I use "kindom" here, rather than "kingdom," to better reflect the communal framework of God's promised world, in which we are all recognized as kin to one another.
12. Elie Wiesel, "The Sacrifice of Isaac: A Survivor's Story," in *Messengers of God* (New York: Simon & Schuster, 1985), 75.
13. Wiesel, "Sacrifice," 83.

## Chapter 4: The Gift of Tension

1. "Abaq," BibleHub, accessed January 9, 2019, https://biblehub.com/hebrew/79.htm.

2. Layton E. Williams, "Out of the Ashes," *Sojourners*, March 2018, https://sojo.net/magazine/march-2018/out-ashes.

## Chapter 6: The Gift of Vulnerability

1. TED, which stands for "Technology, Entertainment, and Design," began as a conference in 1984 and has grown into a global presence. Its primary purpose is to share "ideas worth spreading" via talks given around the world, which are posted online. TEDx talks are locally organized TED events.
2. Jenny Rogers, "What Happens When You Ask Women for Their Stories of Assault? Thousands of Replies," *Washington Post*, October 8, 2016, https://www.washingtonpost.com/posteverything/wp/2016/10/08/what-happens-when-you-ask-women-for-their-stories-of-assault-eight-million-replies/.
3. Layton E. Williams, "How Can Survivors of Abuse Survive This Election Season?," *Sojourners*, October 20, 2016, https://sojo.net/articles/surviving-survivorhood-election-season.

## Chapter 7: The Gift of Trouble

1. David Shedden, "Today in Media History: Mr. Dooley: 'The Job of the Newspaper Is to Comfort the Afflicted and Afflict the Comfortable,'" Poynter Institute, October 7, 2014, https://www.poynter.org/news/today-media-history-mr-dooley-job-newspaper-comfort-afflicted-and-afflict-comfortable.
2. "Tarassō," BibleHub.com, https://biblehub.com/greek/5015.htm.
3. Layton Williams, "Why Is Jesus Sleeping?" (sermon, Fourth Presbyterian Church, Chicago, June 21, 2015), http://fourthchurch.org/sermons/2015/062115_4pm.html.
4. Jamar A. Boyd II, "America Still Doesn't Care about Black and Brown Bodies," *Sojourners*, August 1, 2018, https://sojo.net/articles/america-still-doesnt-care-about-black-and-brown-bodies.
5. Kenya Downs, "When Black Death Goes Viral, It Can Trigger PTSD-Like Trauma," *PBS NewsHour*, July 22, 2016, https://www.pbs.org/newshour/nation/black-pain-gone-viral-racism-graphic-videos-can-create-ptsd-like-trauma.
6. Maureen Callahan, "White Hollywood Only Knows How to Tell Stories about Black Pain," *New York Post*, May 29, 2016, https://nypost.com/2016/05/29/old-ideas-enslave-hollywood/.
7. Sherronda J. Brown, "Decolonizing Empathy: Why Our Pain Will Never Be Enough to Disarm White Supremacy," Black Youth Project, November 13, 2017, http://blackyouthproject.com/decolonizing-empathy-why-pain-never-enough-disarm-white-supremacy/.

## Chapter 8: The Gift of Protest

1. Joe Sommerlad, "Tiananmen Square Massacre: Who Was the Tank Man and How Is He Being Remembered Today?," *Independent*, June 4, 2018, https://

www.independent.co.uk/news/world/asia/tiananmen-square-massacre
-anniversary-beijing-tank-man-china-protests-facts-death-toll-a8382111
.html.

2. Franklin Sherman, "Dietrich Bonhoeffer," *Encyclopaedia Britannica*, December 13, 2018, https://www.britannica.com/biography/Dietrich-Bonhoeffer.

3. Michael Berenbaum, "T4 Program," *Encyclopaedia Britannica*, September 10, 2018, https://www.britannica.com/event/T4-Program.

4. Ryan Stewart, "9 Bonhoeffer Quotes to Remember a Pastor Who Resisted Evil unto Death," *Sojourners*, April 8, 2016, https://sojo.net/articles/11 -bonhoeffer-quotes-remember-pastor-who-resisted-evil-unto-death.

5. Stewart, "Bonhoeffer Quotes."

6. Theological Declaration of Barmen, in *The Constitution of the Presbyterian Church (U.S.A.)*, Part I, *Book of Confessions* (Louisville, KY: Office of the General Assembly, 2004), 8.01–.28.

7. Clifford J. Green, *Bonhoeffer: A Theology of Sociality* (Grand Rapids: Wm. B. Eerdmans Publishing Co., 1999), 241.

8. Stewart, "Bonhoeffer Quotes."

9. Renate Bethge and Christian Gremmels, *Dietrich Bonhoeffer: A Life in Pictures* (Minneapolis: Fortress Press, 2006), 79.

10. History.com editors, "Martin Luther King Jr.," History.com, November 9, 2009, https://www.history.com/topics/black-history/martin-luther-king-jr.

11. Christopher Klein, "10 Things You May Not Know about Martin Luther King Jr.," History.com, last modified January 22, 2019, https://www.history .com/news/10-things-you-may-not-know-about-martin-luther-king-jr.

12. "Letter from Birmingham Jail," April 16, 1963, The Martin Luther King, Jr., Research and Education Institute, https://swap.stanford.edu /20141218232316/http://mlk-kpp01.stanford.edu/kingweb/popular_ requests/.

13. "Public Statement by Eight Alabama Clergymen," April 12, 1963, MassResistance, https://www.massresistance.org/docs/gen/09a/mlk_day/statement .html.

14. Rita Nakashima Brock and Rebecca Ann Parker, *Proverbs of Ashes: Violence, Redemptive Suffering, and the Search for What Saves Us* (Boston: Beacon Press, 2001).

15. "William J. Barber II: We Have to Dare to Preach the Gospel," interview by Jonathan Wilson-Hartgrove, *Faith and Leadership*, October 18, 2016, https://www.faithandleadership.com/william-j-barber-ii-we-have-dare -preach-gospel.

## Chapter 9: The Gift of Hunger

1. Lynne Twist, *The Soul of Money: Transforming Your Relationship with Money and Life* (New York: W. W. Norton, 2017), quoted in Richard Rohr, OFM, "Myth of Scarcity," Center for Action and Contemplation, July 6, 2018, https://cac.org/myth-of-scarcity-2018-07-06/.

2. Larry Elliott, "World's Eight Richest People Have Same Wealth as Poorest 50%," *Guardian*, January 16, 2017, https://www.theguardian.com/global-development/2017/jan/16/worlds-eight-richest-people-have-same-wealth-as-poorest-50.
3. Lura N. Groen, Facebook, November 12, 2018, https://www.facebook.com/lura.groen/posts/10155951167786662

## Chapter 10: The Gift of Limitations

1. Mary Hoffman, *Amazing Grace* (New York: Dial Books for Young Readers, 1991).
2. "Kensington's Beacon," Presbyterian Historical Society, January 12, 2017, https://www.history.pcusa.org/blog/2017/01/kensingtons-beacon.

## Chapter 12: The Gift of Uncertainty

1. "Ranier Maria Rilke," Wikiquote, last modified September 22, 2018, https://en.wikiquote.org/wiki/Rainer_Maria_Rilke.
2. Katherine Lee Baker, Bertram Johnson, Cynthia L. Rigby, Glen Bell, Chris Currie, Brandon Frick, Layton E. Williams, and Jessica Tate, "The Sarasota Statement," NEXT Church, https://nextchurch.net/the-sarasota-statement/sarasota-statement-text/.
3. "Prophets of a Future Not Our Own," United States Conference of Catholic Bishops, http://www.usccb.org/prayer-and-worship/prayers-and-devotions/prayers/prophets-of-a-future-not-our-own.cfm.

CPSIA information can be obtained
at www.ICGtesting.com
Printed in the USA
FSHW011533111019
62934FS

9 780664 265663